DELICIOUS *Rose-*

Flavored DESSERTS

DELICIOUS *Rose-Flavored* DESSERTS

A Modern and Fragrant Take on Classic Recipes

JUDY C. POLINSKY
FOREWORD BY CLAIR G. MARTIN
PHOTOGRAPHS BY BONNIE MATTHEWS

Skyhorse Publishing

Skyhorse Publishing books may be purchased in bulk at special discounts for sales promotion, corporate gifts, fund-raising, or educational purposes. Special editions can also be created to specifications. For details, contact the Special Sales Department, Skyhorse Publishing, 307 West 36th Street, 11th Floor, New York, NY 10018 or info@skyhorsepublishing.com.

Skyhorse® and Skyhorse Publishing® are registered trademarks of Skyhorse Publishing, Inc.®, a Delaware corporation.

Visit our website at www.skyhorsepublishing.com.

10 9 8 7 6 5 4 3 2 1

Library of Congress Cataloging-in-Publication Data is available on file.

Cover design by Laura Klynstra
Cover photo credit Radford Polinsky

Print ISBN: 978-1-5107-0331-5
Ebook ISBN: 978-1-5107-0332-2

Printed in China

This book is dedicated to the memory of two amazing, wonderful individuals, my parents Irv and Millie, who instilled in me a sense of adventure and a great joy for life.

Contents

Foreword

Few plants elicit as strong of an emotional and cultural response as the rose. Slicing across cultural lines, the rose has become an icon. In the West, its use has become almost ubiquitous. "Rose-colored glasses" or "rosy cheeked" are among the many daily uses of the word. Try thinking about Valentine's or Mother's Day without picturing a rose in your mind's eye!

Our strong attachment to the flower is due to its fragrance and our long use of the shrub as a garden flower. It is almost like we are born with the knowledge of what a rose should be etched into our synapses. Watch a young child in the rose garden run from brightly colored and perfumed bloom to bloom, and know that this is in our genes.

For me personally, the use of roses in cooking is virgin territory. Sure, in my studies I had come across recipes using roses from time to time, but in my mind I associated these culinary uses with gingham-frocked 1950s housewives offering trays of homemade cookies—not something a true, red-blooded rosarian should take seriously! Cooking with roses was outside my focus (or so I thought).

Judy Polinsky dragged me kicking and screaming into a world where rose appreciation takes on a new meaning. She seduced me with rose almond cookies and rose-petaled ice cream and her decadent chocolate rose cakes.

Judy began by volunteering in The Huntington Herb Garden but soon followed her nose into my rosy domain. She challenged me to recommend the most fragrant roses for possible use in creating rose waters to use in her culinary experiments. My resistance was weakened and finally breached when she started sharing her rose treats with us in the garden. Once introduced to her eighteenth century pound cake, I was hooked!

Judy's fascination with period cooking mirrors the expansion of roses being developed in Holland and France in the eighteenth century. While in the early part of the century roses remained the hobby of the aristocracy, by the end ordinary citizens were discovering the joys of growing roses in their home gardens. Often the most popular roses were also the most fragrant. Those were ripe, smelly times, and one couldn't just pick up a room deodorizer at the corner apothecary nor could you find rose water at the local grocer. If you wanted to jazz up your grandmother's pound cake, you had to make your own rose water.

This book is a product of Judy's determination and perseverance promoting roses in cooking. A few years back, I invited her to share some of her treats at the Great Rosarians of the World™ annual lecture series at The Huntington. Her rose cookies and cakes expanded to rose-flavored puddings and whipped cream, and she seduced a new audience into her world of rose cooking. Those of us who were privileged to be her test subjects soon came to the universal opinion that she needed to write a book, and this is the product of all those experiments.

Enjoy!

Clair G. Martin
Curator Emeritus of the
Huntington Rose Garden
San Marino, California

Little Almond Cakes

Blanch one pound of almonds
in boiling water, beat them
in a mortar with a little
rosewater; when they are
fine, add to them half a
pound of

Introduction

Have you ever imagined a table laden with sweet dishes? Cakes, puddings, creams, custards, jellies, candied fruits, marzipan, ice creams molded into exotic forms, all served as the final course of your meal? I have! After reading Georgian era cookbooks as an amateur historian, I became curious about the economic, political, and social factors that would create an entire table of sweets as a show of wealth and power. This is the fascination that led me to research more about Georgian food, particularly the dessert course.

I am intrigued by the use of roses and rose water in Georgian foods. The result is this book of recipes (or as the Georgians wrote "receipts"). The eighteenth century original receipt is printed on the left-hand page, facing the modern version on the right-hand page. In deciphering eighteenth century text or personal handwriting, I have attempted to stay true to the receipts and the cook's knowledge and skills. Each receipt was tested without the use of any electric conveniences, all by hand, then retested using modern appliances such as mixers and food processors. The results will vary slightly. If the entire receipt is mixed by hand, the result will be a denser version than the modern palate is accustomed to. However, the reward is in the subtle blending and mixing of unexpected flavors to create a wonderful treat.

Whether your interest is in cooking, rose gardening, or history, using roses from your garden to recreate unusual recipes is an adventure and great fun!

Rose Cream
(see pg. 141)

Roses and Food

"The perfume of roses are
like exquisite chords of music
composed of many orderd
notes harmoniously blended."
—N. F. Miller

For centuries, rose water has been used in wines, medicines, clothing, baths and bed linens, personal fragrance, and food preparation. Why have roses been used in so many ways over the centuries? Because the rose entices us with its scent and captivates us with its beauty. We want to capture and savor it.

The Chinese were growing roses before the birth of Christ. The Assyrian king Sargon brought roses to Ur in Babylon in 717 BC. When King Cyrus of Persia captured Babylon in 539 BC, he brought and tended roses in his own garden. By the sixth century, Persia was a land of roses. Rose plantations were planted, most notable of which was the one at Gulistan. This garden was so large, it took five days to ride through it. From these roses, attar (rose oil) was produced— rose oil for the Sultan's use—and petals for the royal beds. The rose has been used in designs on Persian miniature paintings, porcelain, carpets, and tapestries for centuries.

King Midas brought shrub roses to Greece from Persia, according to the historian Herodotus (485-25 BC), who visited his garden in Asia Minor. One of the earliest references to the use of the rose was from Homer's *Iliad*, where he writes that it is the perfume oil with which the dead Hector is rubbed. By the fifth century, the Greeks were cultivating roses in their gardens and using them for decorative purposes, personal and otherwise, on festive occasions.

The Romans produced skilled gardeners. Pliny (c. AD 77) recorded the wealth of aromatics in his work, *Natural History*, which gave elementary descriptions of the twelve roses of his time. Pliny also wrote of the medicinal use of roses, noting thirty-two remedies for which the rose was used. The Romans began the myth that persisted into the seventeenth century that roses prevented drunkenness. "They ate rose pâtés, rose jellies, rose honey, and rose puddings decorated with candied rose petals. Their houses and tables were strewn with roses, lovers exchanged rose wreaths, and at dances, the slaves, flute-players, and dancers all wore crowns of roses. The Romans put rose blossoms into their bath water to help preserve the skin, and after bathing massaged each other's bodies with rose ointments."[1] With their conquests and colonization, the Romans brought roses from their gardens to Western Europe. With the fall of the Roman Empire, power and perfume passed to the Eastern Empire.

Byzantium was a scented splendor, its ports the center of the scent trade, holding all the fragrances of the East. The Arabs became the perfumers of the world. Through their vast networks, Arab and Persian merchants made spices from isolated areas of Asia available to the cultures of the Mediterranean. The Middle East devotees planted old shrub roses from Persia to recreate their faith's Paradise garden. "Paradise" is derived from the Persian word for garden. The rose was cultivated for the production of rose water and medicinal use. It was here that one of the most important discoveries in the world of perfume occurred: alcohol. The discovery that the aroma of plants could be extracted

---

[1] Rosamond Richardson, *Roses: A Celebration* (London: Platkus, 1984), 14.

Rose Water Ices
(see pg. 163)

and preserved by a distillation process made modern perfumes possible. Prior to this discovery, scents had to be incorporated either into a wine base or into an oily mass. It was Avicenna, the great physician, philosopher, and scientist (who lived from 980–1036 AD), who invented distillation and, with it, the modern perfume. For his first experiment, he chose the Arabs' favorite flower: the rose. He succeeded in extracting a perfume that is still a favorite the world over—rose water. Rose water was used as a flavoring for sherbets and confections, and rose oil was used on the skin and hair.

Rose water, as well as other Eastern perfumes, was brought back to Europe by the Christian knights returning from the Crusades. It was noted that Middle Eastern women freely anointed themselves with these exotic scents. These new perfumes intrigued the knights. To France, the Crusaders brought roses and rose legends back from the Middle East, and rose gardens were created. This was the reintroduction of perfumes into Europe

on a scale that had been unknown since Roman times. Most of the perfumes were imported from the Middle East, but local businesses quickly began to recreate these new scents. By the end of the twelfth century, local manufacturers were supplying their own products—conserves and confections, oils, rose water, rose honey, and rose vinegars—to the women of France. These manufacturers were important and in such numbers that King Philip Augustus granted them charters in 1190. For the most part, these perfumers reproduced the traditional scents of the Middle East.

During the Dark Ages, the rose had been banned from early Christian churchyards due to its association with pagan cults. With the passing of the Dark Ages, the rose regained favor. Damasks, Gallicas, and Albas, as well as a few wild roses, were grown in enclosed rose gardens, often formal in plan, featuring fountains, walls, and arbors with roses cascading down. The roses caught the medieval imagination; poems and songs extolled the virtues of this flower. Roses appeared in paintings, tapestries, and architectural features, as well as adorning clothing. Late in eleventh-century England, the rose appeared as a heraldic motif.

Venice was the European leader in trade for much of the Middle Ages and the early Renaissance. It was also the first place where imported goods and newly refined tastes appeared. Italian gardens of the Renaissance had rose hedges, creating a garden within a garden. It was here that roses were grown not just for decoration but also for use in medicine, herbals, and cosmetics. In the sixteenth century, the Italians led the Western world in perfumery.

The fashion for lavish application of scent was brought from Italy to England during the reign of Elizabeth I. On returning from a visit to Italy, the Earl of Oxford brought back the Italian court fashion of wearing scented gloves. The Queen owned numerous pairs of scented gloves and spent extravagantly on perfumes. Elizabeth I was fascinated by perfumes of all kinds. Notably, one of her favorite scents was made of musk and roses. It was during this time

that commercial gardens were planted for the production of rose oil. Around 1540, another type of garden was first recorded in sixteenth-century London: the first botanic or "physic" gardens, emulating those Italian gardens of Pisa and Padua. Britain's first collection of roses grew in Oxford's Botanic Gardens.

During the latter part of the eighteenth century, the landscape gardener Humphrey Repton created a new type of garden. He planted flowers bordering the stately homes of his aristocratic employers. His rosarium at Ashridge Park in Hertfordshire was one of the first proper English rose gardens. During the late eighteenth century, the English grew mainly Gallicas, Centifolias, Damask, and Moss roses, but the nineteenth-century boom in rose nurseries was to change all that.

Empress Josephine, wife of Napoleon I, was an ardent admirer of the rose. At her estate, Chateau Malmaison, varieties from all over the world were collected, cultivated, and bred with new scientific techniques. The gardens had over two

Begger's Pudding
(see pg. 149)

hundred varieties. It was here that the rose blossomed into the preeminent flower it is today. Rose gardens were soon an essential accessory to the estates of the wealthy.

Beginning in Tudor England and continuing well into the early nineteenth century, roses and rose water were widely used in both sweet and savory dishes. Period recipes show that roses and rose water were ingredients of cakes, puddings, ice creams, conserves, creams, sauces, and syllabubs.

As the British Empire expanded (after 1660), sugar became more available. As an indication of how greatly the British public desired sugar, three sugar cones on a sign was the mark of a grocer's shop. Sugar was sold in cone-shaped forms and crushed for use at home. The demand for sugar also rose, in part, because it served as an important preserving agent; apples, pears, peaches, berries, rose petals, and herbs could be made into cordials, preserves, or candies. It was a way to keep the fresh produce of the summer harvest well into the year.

The expansion of trade also introduced new varieties of foods, fruits, and spices: cinnamon, cloves, East Indian pepper, capers, caviar, anchovies, olives, ginger, chocolate, and nutmeg, as well as mangos, pineapples, and bananas. Reflecting the experience of the Englishman abroad, British cuisine showed influences from the French, Spanish, Italian, German, Portuguese, Dutch, Indian, and West Indian cultures. Britain had a strong native tradition of cooking which relied on foreign imports and now a rapidly growing world trade. Cooks were creating new dishes. The Georgian period was ripe with culinary potential, and its cooks began experimenting and writing.

Specialty books began to appear. One such was *The Compleat Confectioner, The Pastry Cook's Vademecum: The Court and Country Confectioner* (London, 1770) by a Mr. Borella, who was head confectioner to the Spanish Ambassador in England. This book lures the reader in with descriptions of cakes, custards, creams, candies, jellies, puffs, flummeries, trifles, preserves, knickknacks, syllabubs, and punches. Cookbooks influenced the desire of the status conscious to be up to date. Other important confectionary books were John Nott's *Cook and Confectioner's Dictionary* (1723) and *Receipts of Pastry & Cookery for the Use of His Scholars* by Edward Kidder (1720-1740?). These books fueled the British passion for sweets!

While earlier cookbooks did exist, the Georgian period saw a proliferation of cookbooks not just dedicated to the wealthy but to the rising middle class who sought to emulate their betters. During the early part of the eighteenth century, two groups of cookbook authors evolved: the male chefs who cooked for the aristocracy or for the royals, and women authors who worked for the gentry as cooks or housekeepers or were housewives themselves. The best examples are the works of Hannah Glasse (*The Art of Cookery Made Plain and Easy; Which Far Exceeds Any Thing of the Kind Yet Published*, 1747), John Farley (*The London Art of Cookery*), Elizabeth Raffald, (*The Experienced English Housekeeper*, 1769),

and Eliza Smith (*The Compleat Housewife*, 1727). These cookbooks are among a number that were published in multiple editions and were vastly successful. There was a second more private tradition of personal or family collections of recipes. A cook would record his recipes in a notebook or journal, then pass it on to his heir and so on. One, two, and sometimes multiple sets of handwriting in the same private notebooks and diaries are evidence of this. *The Georgian Cookery Book* is the published journal of Margaretta Acworth. Spanning seventy years of cooking, it had been passed down from her mother, Anne Ball.

Britain's aristocrats used lavish splendor to demonstrate their wealth, status, and political strength. The dining table was evidence of that. Elegance and overly elaborate formality were key to establishing a social pecking order. Until the middle of the eighteenth century, food in upper class households was consumed in a seated buffet known as the French style of presentation. When entertaining or at holiday dinners, a meal would consist of a number of

Caraway Cake
(see pg. 43)

courses comprised of up to twenty dishes all on the table at the same time. Diners helped themselves. The number of dishes per course would be dependent on the economic status of the household. Toward the end of the eighteenth century, this style of dining changed to what was called the Russian service. Individual dishes and their accompaniments were served in a series of courses, each cleared away before the next arrived. It was not unusual to have two or three courses, each comprised of ten to fifteen different dishes encompassing both sweets and savories included in each course, ending with a sweet course. Much of eighteenth-century culture is about "show" and consumption of material goods. Providing an extraordinary and exotic, expensive meal was an acceptable way to prove your status in the social hierarchy. An extravagant dessert course ending your meal was a notable symbol of wealth.

An eighteenth-century British newspaper, *The London Tradesman*, wrote that a confectioner "delights the Eye . . . as much as the Taste." "Between 1700 and 1800 Britain's annual sugar consumption rose more than 350 percent from four pounds per head to thirteen."[2] Initially sugar was only available to the rich, but with the establishment of the West Indies plantations, sugar became more affordable by mid-century. An important upper class dinner might have a fanciful centerpiece: a building, a castle, an entire garden—built of spun sugar and sweetmeats. Puddings, pies, little cakes, flummeries, custards, tarts, syllabubs, marzipan, candied fruits, and sweetmeats graced the upper class tables arranged around these sugar fantasy centerpieces.

One new treat appeared in confectionary shops—ice cream, colored and molded into fanciful shapes (grapes, apples, birds, fish, a cathedral, etc.). The confectioner's shop was a place where you could purchase these ice creams and sugared treats in many new exotic flavors, such as parmesan

[2] Sandra Sherman, Fresh from the Past, Recipes and Revelations from Moll Flanders' Kitchen (Lanham, MD: Taylor Trade Publishing, 2004), 263, 264.

Whitpot
(see pg. 167)

cheese, rose, white coffee, brown bread, as well as berry flavors, even in winter. Few ordinary people could preserve ice to make these new ice creams fresh. So to make an impression on dinner guests, one bought these new treats at the confectioner's. The aristocrats, as a sign of wealth and fashion, began to build ice houses in their gardens, the better to have ice at the ready for social occasions.

Fortunately for the modern reader, you don't have to be an aristocrat to create delightful confections! Sugar, roses, and ice are all readily available for those who, like me, wish to explore and rediscover the joy and delight of cooking with roses!

Selecting Your Roses

Wander through your garden early in the morning. Breathe in the fragrance of each rose. Every rose has its own unique scent and flavor. Choose the roses that beckon you to them, the ones that entice you to pick them and revel in their aroma. Let your nose be your guide!

Choose fresh flowers with a deep, rich bouquet. After testing hundreds of roses, both antique and modern, my research has shown that the fragrance of deep reds and pinks picked early in the morning remains more true to their scent when making rose water. Make sure there is no mold or black spot on your roses.

The parentage of a rose will help determine if it will produce a good rose water.

Rosa gallica was one of the first roses to be cultivated in the Middle East. Grown throughout the Roman Empire, it was the rose brought to England from Gaul. *Rosa gallica* was the rose of medieval gardens and the parent of the Apothecary's Rose; *R. gallica officinalis,* also known as the Rose of Provins. "By 1600 the main street of Provins was peopled with apothecaries who made conserves and confections, oils, rose water, rose honey and rose vinegar—all from this highly aromatic rose . . ."[3] Examples of some of my favorites include these:

- (Apothecary Rose)
- Empress Josephine

[3] Rosamond Richardson, *Roses: A Celebration* (London: Platkus, 1984), 39.

- Rosa Officinalis
- Rosa Mundi
- Tuscany

Rosa centifolia was bred either by the French or the Dutch, who produced many Centifolia hybrids during the seventeenth century. *Rosa centifolia* was also known as the Provence rose or Cabbage rose. This is a parent of the Moss rose, *R. muscosa*, a highly scented shrub rose. *R. centifolia* was introduced into England during the reign of William and Mary, where it remained a favorite until the end of the nineteenth century. Still, it was during the Georgian period in England that we see the greatest use of rose water in English foods, notably their cakes, custards and puddings, as well as some savory dishes. Cultivated varieties include these:

- Red Provence
- Rosa Centifolia Bullata
- Rose de Meaux

Rosa damascena was taken by the Greeks from Damascus to their trade centers, as far away as Marseilles and Carthage. The parentage of this ancient rose, lost in the mists of time, is known as the Summer Damask.

R. damascena x *bifera*, the Autumn Damask, is the offspring of *R. gallica* and *R. moschata*, flowering twice: once in summer and again in autumn. This is the only rose in the pre-nineteenth-century world to flower twice a year. *R. damascena* is a parent, along with *R. canina*, of *Rosa alba*, the white rose of York. In early June, these Damask roses offer a lovely fragrance and a strong scent, which makes a good rose water:

- Kazanlik
- Konigin von Danemark
- Leda
- Mme. Hardy
- White Rose of York

R. moschata is called the Musk rose, due to its scent. The offspring of *R. gallica* and the Phoenician musk rose, it was brought from the Middle East to Europe by the Christian monks. Thomas Cromwell was thought to have brought it from Italy to England in 1513. *R. moschata* is fragrant but can add bitterness to the rose water due to its musky odor. A good example of this rose family is Old Double Musk (Rosa muschata).

At the end of the eighteenth century, the *Rosa chinensis* made its way to the West. By 1781, the Dutch were growing China roses, and by the 1790s, these were popular in England and America. This rose is the ancestor of today's Hybrid Teas, Floribundas, Climbers, Ramblers, Shrubs, and miniatures. These examples are heavy bloomers, which give you more roses to work with:

- Old Blush
- Slater's China

When *R. chinensis* was crossed with *R. gallica*, it produced the Hybrid China; crossing this with Portland, Damasks, and Bourbons produced the first Hybrid Perpetuals. They are a small shrub, highly scented and robust, usually dark red or deep pink in color. They are repeat bloomers. From 1840 to 1890, these were favorites in English gardens:

- American Beauty
- Baronne Prevost
- Mrs. John Laing
- Paul Neyron
- Reine des Violettes

Tea roses, *R. odorata*, are a cross between *R. chinensis* and *R. gigantea* and may also have Musk rose, *R. moschata*, in their history. Their scent is delicate; they have a lovely form and display a soft coloration. This rose was quite popular in the nineteenth century. Unfortunately, they are not very hardy in cold winter regions. Lightly scented versions for a delicate rose water are the following:

- Etoile de Lyon
- Francis du Breuil
- Lady Hillingdon
- Maman Coche
- Safrano

In 1867, a Tea rose was crossed with a Hybrid Perpetual to create "La France," the first Hybrid Tea. It was hardy and had a long flowering season. The scent was mild but not exceptional. Over the years, breeders have been cross-breeding to develop more scent in the modern Hybrid Tea. These Hybrid Teas fostered rose gardens with long flowering seasons and added numerous colors. The following are fragrant enough and make a nice rose water:

- Barcelona
- Baron Edmund de Rothschild
- The Doctor
- Double Delight
- Tiffany
- Mister Lincoln
- Oklahoma
- Chrysler Imperial
- The McCartney Rose

R. multiflora was introduced in the nineteenth century from China and Japan. It had single white clustered flowers and was a hardy climber. This led the way to the Polyantha climbers and Poly Pompoms. Following this, *R. wichuraiana*, a rambling rose from Japan, was introduced. This, too, had single white flowers. When *R. wichuraiana* was crossed *with R. multiflora* and hybrid Teas, many of today's ramblers were the result, including these:

- Alberic Barbier
- Alexander Girault
- Dorothy Perkins

Floribundas were developed in the mid-twentieth century. They are easy to grow, disease-resistant, and come in a wide range of colors, with a growing season from summer through autumn. Svend Poulsen of Denmark crossed Poly Pompoms with Hybrid Teas to create the Floribundas. Here are some Floribundas I have tested for rose waters:

- Iceberg
- Pink Bountiful
- Love Potion
- Heaven on Earth
- Rose Parade

Miniature roses, bred from *R. chimensis munima* are miniatures of their larger ancestors, having first appeared in Europe in the late eighteenth century. Unlike their larger siblings, these miniatures are quite hardy. Though many are fragrant, a great deal of work is required to use them to make rose water since the petals are so tiny.

These two are worth the effort:

- Beauty Secret
- Sweet Fairy

Shrub roses that make a fragrant rose water include these:

- Dark Lady
- Gertrude Jekyll
- Munstead Wood

Commercial versus Homemade Rose Water

Rose waters differ in character. Commercial rose water is usually made of a blend of different roses distilled together. For many people, this can lead to the rose water having a very strong, almost soapy flavor, so use commercial rose water sparingly. On the other hand, homemade rose water allows you more control of flavor. Using a single rose variety to make rose water makes for a very pleasant aroma (like the rose you use). When using homemade rose water in these recipes, the scent and flavor will be milder than commercial, so you will need to add two, three, or even four times the quantity. Let your nose be your guide—you should be able to smell the rose water in the batter! Don't worry; since they're water-based, most of the extra liquid evaporates in the baking, and the recipe does not have to be altered for the extra liquid. Turn the page for instructions on how to make your own rose water at home.

Making Rose Water

Making rose water is as easy as making sun tea! The most important safety factor to remember is to make sure that the roses you pick have not been sprayed with insecticide, fungicide, or any other pesticides for at least six to nine months.

You will need:

Roses with enough fresh, clean
    petals to fill your chosen
    container halfway
2 Mason or canning jars—very
    clean (any size)
1 funnel
1 coffee filter that fits the funnel
Vodka (unflavored)

1. Pick your roses early in the morning when they are most fragrant!
2. Choose roses that are newly opened and fresh looking, making sure there is *no mold or black spot* on the petals.
3. Quickly rinse the petals in cool water, and pat dry.
4. Once you have pulled the petals from the flower, cut off the small triangular-shaped and usually different-colored base of the petal. This base is quite bitter and will affect the taste of your rose water.
5. Place the petals in a clean jar. No matter what size jar you use, fill with petals at least halfway up the container. The more petals you use, the stronger your rose water will be.

6. For a pint jar, pour 2–3½ teaspoons (two or three capfuls) of unflavored vodka into the petal-filled jar. For other-sized jars, adjust as necessary.

7. Pour boiling water over the petals, filling the jar to the top.

8. Tightly close the lid on the jar, and shake the jar a few times.

9. Put the filled jar in the sun for three or four days, shaking the jar once or twice a day to shift the contents around, allowing the sun's rays to get to all the rose petals.

10. Place a funnel (lined with a coffee filter) into a clean jar. Using the filtered funnel, pour the contents of the petal-filled jar into the filter within the second jar, petals and all. Once you have poured it all out, squeeze the filter with the rose petals into the new jar to get every last drop of your new rose water from the petals. Be sure that none of the petals fall out of the filter and into the new jar.

11. If you are using it within the week, store the rose water in your refrigerator. Otherwise, freeze the rose water for later use. Freezing the rose water will allow you to keep it indefinitely. If you store it in the refrigerator and see any signs of mold, DO NOT use the rose water.

Now it is your turn to try rose water store-bought or your own infusion. The rewards of having made your own are that, with each individual rose you use to make your rose water, that rose's unique fragrance and taste will be quite evident. You can make the same recipe a number of times, trying different varieties of the rose to create the rose water, and each time, the taste will be different!

Prussian Cake
(see pg. 57)

Cakes

Cakes are made with a raised or aerated batter. Over the course of the eighteenth century, cake recipes saw the increased use of a great number of eggs as a raising agent instead of yeast or barm (the froth or foam that rises to the top of fermenting liquor). It could take up to two hours of beating to get a batter to rise! There were also confectioner's shops where one could purchase cakes and sweets to feed the Englishman's growing appetite for sugar!

Biscuit Cake
41

Caraway Cake
43

Gingerbread Cake
45

Lemon Cake
47

Nun's Cake or a Rich Seed Cake
49

Orange Cake
51

Plumb Cake
53

Pound Cake
55

Prussian Cake
57

Rose Water Pound Cake
59

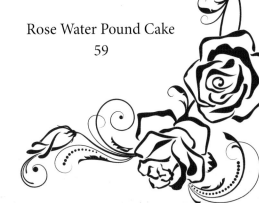

Biscuit Cake

Whisk the whites of ten eggs to light froth, put in the yolks, and beat them a little, then add a pound of double refined sugar beaten and sifted; beat it well together for 20 minutes, then add three quarters of a pound of flour, the rind of one lemon rasped and chopt, add a little rose-water; beat it together for a quarter of an hour, and bake it in a quick oven.

—*The Compleat Housewife: or,*
Accomplished Gentlewoman's Companion,
Eliza Smith, p. 256 (1728)

Biscuit Cake

This half recipe yields about 36 little cakes (cookies).

5 egg whites (beaten)
5 egg yolks
½ cup sifted sugar
¾ cup flour
1 lemon rind, rasped and chopped
½ tablespoon rose water

1. Whisk the egg whites until frothy, add the yolks, and beat a little.
2. Add the sugar, and beat well.
3. Add the flour, lemon rind, and rose water, and beat well.
4. Drop by tablespoons onto parchment paper.
5. Bake at 375°F for 6–9 minutes until you see a very slight browning on the edge.

A Quick Note About Eggs

In a number of recipes, I say to use medium-sized eggs. I tested the recipes using both large and medium eggs; there is a difference! In the eighteenth century, eggs were smaller. A medium egg is closer to the historic size, and some recipes do not work well if you use large eggs. If you can't find medium eggs, just remember that one large egg is equal to one and a half medium eggs, and adjust the number of eggs in the recipe.

A Very Good Carraway Cake

Dry three Pounds of the best Flour before the Fire, then divide it into two Parts; on one Part grate one Nutmeg, put two Spoonfuls of Rose-water, or Sack, the Yolks of four Eggs, as must Ale Yeast as will make it into Paste, and let it lie and rise in the Warmth of the Fire, 'till it's as light as Cork; then take the other half of the Flour, and break into it a Pound of Butter, very small, a little new Milk, luke-warm; make the Flour and Butter into a Paste; then take the two Pastes, and break them together, and strew in a Pound of smooth Caraway Seeds, and mix them well together, then make up the Cake, and bake it in a Hoop, or Paper, and strew over it double refin'd Sugar, and rough Carraway Seeds, Let the Oven be not too hot, and a little more than an Hour will bake it.

—*The Art of Cookery*
Hannah Glasse, pp. 369–370 (1753)

Caraway Cake

½ cup + 1 tablespoon softened butter, divided

2½ cups flour

1 teaspoon baking powder

Pinch of salt

¾ cup sugar

1 tablespoon caraway seeds

1 medium-size egg

½ cup milk

½ teaspoon rose water

1. Preheat oven to 350°F. With 1 tablespoon of softened butter, grease then flour the bottom and sides of an 8-inch pan.
2. Sift together 2½ cups flour with the salt and baking powder.
3. In a separate bowl, cream together ½ cup butter and the sugar. Mix in the caraway seeds and egg. Add the flour mixture, milk, and rose water, beating well.
4. Pour batter into prepared cake pan.
5. Bake for 55 minutes or until a knife inserted into the center comes out clean. Cool.

Gingerbread

Three pound flour, two pound sugar, one pound butter, one ounce carraway seed, one ounce ginger, nine eggs, one glass rose-water, milk sufficient to make it of a proper consistence.

—*American Cookery*,
Amelia Simmons, p. 50 (1796)

Gingerbread Cake

1 cup (8 ounces) butter at room temperature

2 cups (1 pound) sugar

5 eggs

2 tablespoons (½ ounce) caraway seeds

3 tablespoons (½ ounce) dried ginger or 2 tablespoons fresh ginger

¼ cup rose water

5 cups flour

1 cup buttermilk

1. Cream butter lightly. Add the sugar, and continue beating.
2. Add eggs, and beat.
3. Beat in caraway seeds, ginger, and rose water.
4. If flour is lumpy, sift it. Add flour to egg mixture in small amounts, alternating with the buttermilk. The batter will get sticky.
5. Grease and flour a 10-inch tube pan. Gently pour the batter into the pan.
6. Bake in a preheated 350°F oven for 1 hour or until a toothpick inserted comes out clean.

To Make Lemon Cake,
A Second Way

Beat the whites of ten eggs with a whisk for one hour with three spoonfuls of rose or orange flower water, then put in one pound of loaf sugar beat and sifted, with the yellow rind of a lemon grated into it; when it is well mixed put in the juice of half a lemon and the yolks of ten eggs beat smooth, and just before you put it into the oven stir in three quarters of a pound of flour; butter your pan, and one hour will bake it in a moderate oven.

—*The Experienced English Housekeeper*,
Elizabeth Raffald, p. 269 (1776)

Lemon Cake

10 medium egg whites
10 medium egg yolks
3 tablespoons rose water
3 cups sugar
zest of 1 lemon
juice of ½ lemon
2⅔ cups flour

1. Preheat the oven to 350°F.
2. Beat the egg whites and rose water together until soft peaks form (use medium speed on your mixer).
3. In a separate bowl, mix the lemon zest into the sugar. Add this to the egg-white mixture, and mix well.
4. In a separate bowl, beat the egg yolks until smooth.
5. Add the lemon juice and the beaten egg yolks to the sugar and egg-white mixture.
6. Gently stir in the flour.
7. Butter a 12-inch springform pan, pour batter in, and bake at 350°F for about 60 minutes.

Nun's Cake or a Rich Seed Cake

You must take four pounds of the finest flour, and three pounds of double-refined sugar beaten and sifted; mix them together, and dry them by the fire till you prepare the other materials; take four pounds of butter, beat it with your hand till it is soft like cream; then beat thirty-five eggs, leave out sixteen whites, strain off your eggs from the treads, and beat them and the butter together till all appear like butter; put in four or five spoonfuls of rose or orange-flower water, and beat again; then take your flour and sugar, with six ounces of carraway-seeds, and strew them in by degrees, beating it up all the time for two hours together; you may put in as much tincture of cinnamon or ambergris as you please; butter your hoop, and let it stand three hours in a moderate oven. You must observe always, in beating of butter, to do it with a cool hand, and beat it always one way in a deep earthen dish.

—*The Art of Cookery Made Plain and Easy*,
Hannah Glasse, p. 311 (1796)

Nun's Cake or a Rich Seed Cake

1 cup butter, softened
2 whole eggs
2 egg yolks
1 tablespoon rose water
2 cups flour

pinch of salt
½ cup plus 3 tablespoons sugar
¾ teaspoon caraway seeds
good pinch of ground cinnamon

1. Soften the butter, allowing it to come to room temperature. Cream the butter, then beat in the eggs and yolks, one at a time, blending each in thoroughly before adding the next.
2. Mix in the rose water.
3. Sieve together the flour, salt, and sugar, then mix them lightly into the creamed ingredients to make a fairly soft dough.
4. Lastly, add the caraway seeds and cinnamon.
5. Line a 6½-inch cake tin with two layers of parchment paper, and brush lightly with butter. Pour the mixture into the greased pan and smooth the top.
6. Bake at 325°F for 1¼–1½ hours until golden and springy to touch.
7. Cool on a wire rack.

Orange Cake

Take the whites of ten eggs, put to them three spoonfuls of rose, or orange flower water, and beat them an hour with a whisk. Then put in a pound of beaten and sifted sugar, and grate into it the rind of orange. When well mixed, put in the juice of half an orange, and the yolks of ten eggs beaten smooth. Just before putting it into the oven, stir in three quarters of a pound of flour, butter the pan, put it into a moderate oven, and an hour will bake it.

—*The London Art of Cookery and Domestic Housekeeper's Complete Assistant,* John Farley, pp. 276–77 (1811)

Orange Cake

10 egg whites
10 egg yolks (beaten smooth)
3 tablespoons rose water
2 cups sugar (sifted)
1 orange rind (grated)
juice of ½ orange (more if you wish a stronger flavor)
2⅔ cups flour

1. Place the egg whites and rose water in a mixer, and beat to soft peaks.
2. Add the sugar and the orange rind to the beaten egg whites.
3. When well mixed, add the orange juice and the beaten egg yolks.
4. Once combined, stir in the flour.
5. Pour the mixture gently into your well-greased tube pan.
6. Bake at 350°F for about 55–60 minutes. If the cake begins to brown, cover with foil, and continue to bake. Let cool before removing from the pan.

To Make Plumb-cakes Another Way

Take two pounds of butter, beat it with a little rose water and orange-flower-water till it be like cream, two pounds of flour dried before the fire, a quarter of an ounce of mace, a nutmeg, half a pound of loaf sugar beat and sifted, fifteen eggs (beat the whites by themselves and yolks with your sugar) a jack of brandy and as much sack, two pounds of currants very well clean'd, and half a pound of almonds blanch'd and cut in two or three piece length way, so mix all together, and put it into your hoop or tin; you may put in half a pound of candy'd orange and citron if you please; about an hour will bake it in a quick oven; if you have a mind to have it iced a pound of sugar will ice it.

—*English Housewifery,* Elizabeth Moxon,
p. 115 (247), (London 1775)

Plumb Cake

This half recipe will yield one 9-inch cake.

1 pound (4 sticks) butter

1–1¼ tablespoons rose water

1 tablespoon orange-flower water

6 medium egg whites + 1 large egg white

2 cups flour

1 teaspoon mace

6 medium egg yolks + 1 large egg yolk

½ a nutmeg (grated, about a teaspoon)

½ cup sugar (sifted)

1 ounce brandy

1 ounce sack (sherry)

1 cup currants

1 cup almonds, blanched and each cut into 3 pieces

1. Beat the butter with the rose water and orange-flower water until it is pale and creamy.
2. In a separate bowl, beat all the egg whites to soft peaks.
3. In another separate bowl, beat all the egg yolks with the sugar until smooth.
4. To the butter mixture, add the flour, mace, nutmeg, egg yolk and sugar mixture, almonds, brandy, sack, egg whites, and currants. Mix it all together.
5. Put the batter into a 9-inch cake pan, and bake at 325°F for 50–55 minutes. Turn off the oven, leaving the cake in until the cake top becomes golden (an extra 5–8 minutes).

Another (called) Pound Cake

Work three quarters of a pound butter, one pound of good sugar, 'till very white, whip ten whites to a foam, add the yolks and beat together, add one spoon rose water, 2 of brandy, and put the whole to one and a quarter of a pound flour, if yet too soft flour and bake slowly.

—American Cookery,
Amelia Simmons, p. 37 (1796)

Pound Cake

¾ pound (3 sticks) butter

2 cups sugar

10 egg whites (beaten to gentle peaks)

10 egg yolks

½ cup rose water

1 cup brandy

2½ cups flour (add more if too soft)

1. Cream butter until very light.
2. Add sugar, and beat until combined.
3. Add the egg yolks and beaten egg whites, and gently combine—do not overbeat.
4. Add the rose water and brandy; gently beat just until lightly combined.
5. Add the flour, keeping the batter light and fluffy.
6. Gently pour into a greased and floured 10-inch bundt or tube pan.
7. Bake at 350°F for about 1 hour or until a toothpick inserted has a slightly moist crumb.

To make Prussian Cake

Take a pound of sugar beat and sifted, half a pound of flour dried, seven eggs, beat the yolks and white separate, the juice of one lemon, the peel of two grated very fine, half a pound of almonds beat fine with rose water; as soon as the whites are beat to a froth, put in all the things except the flour and beat them together for half an hour, just before you set it in the oven shake in the flour.

   N.B. The whites and yolks must be beat separate, or it will be quite heavy.

—*The Experienced English Housekeeper*,
Elizabeth Raffald, p. 273 (1776)

Prussian Cake

This is a half recipe.

1 tablespoon + 1 teaspoon rose water
2⅓ cups almond flour
juice of ½ lemon (⅜ cup)
1 lemon peel, grated fine and chopped

1 cup sugar
2 medium egg yolks + 1 large egg yolk
2 medium egg whites + 1 large egg white
1 cup flour, sifted

1. Beat the rose water into the almond flour.
2. Beat in the lemon juice, lemon peel, and sugar.
3. In a separate bowl, beat the yolks; then add to mixture.
4. In another separate bowl, beat the egg whites to a froth; then gently incorporate into the mixture.
5. Very gently stir in the sifted flour.
6. *Three choices!* All work well:
   - Pour into an 8-inch springform pan, and bake at 350°F for at least 30 minutes; then, leaving the oven door closed, bake for another 5–8 minutes.
   - Pour into small muffin pans, and bake at 350°F for at least 30 minutes; then, leaving the oven door closed, bake for another 5–8 minutes.
   - Drop onto parchment as a cookie, and bake at 350°F for 12–15 minutes or until the edges just begin to turn fawn-colored.

Rosewater Pound Cake

One pound sugar, one pound butter, one pound flour, ten eggs, rose water one gill, spices to your taste; watch it well, it will bake in a slow oven in 15 minutes.

—*American Cookery*,
Amelia Simmons, p. 48 (1796)

Rose Water Pound Cake

2 cups (1 pound) butter
2 cups (1 pound) sugar
10 eggs
3½ cups flour (sift only if lumpy)
¼–½ cup rose water

1. Preheat oven to 350°F.
2. Cream butter very light.
3. Add the sugar, and continue to beat.
4. Add the eggs, and beat.
5. Add the flour in small amounts to the butter mixture, alternating with the rose water. Make sure the batter stays light and fluffy.
6. Grease and flour a 9-inch tube or bundt pan.
7. Pour batter gently into the pan.
8. Bake at 350°F for 50–60 minutes or until a toothpick inserted comes out with a moist crumb.

Portugal Cakes
(see pg. 85)

Small Cakes

Some small cakes or biscuits are what we call cookies today. Other small cakes were similar to bite-sized modern-day muffins, and some were simply smaller versions of full-sized cakes. They were served at social and festive occasions, and in the mid-eighteenth century, it became fashionable to offer visitors tea with small cakes in the afternoon.

Almond Cheesecakes
65

Butter Drops
67

Common Biscuits
69

Currant and Seed Cakes
71

Drop Biscuits
73

Gingerbread in Little Pans
75

Rose Water–Currant Cakes
77

Little Almond Cakes
79

Little Queen's Cakes
79

Rose Macaroons
83

Portugal Cakes
85

Gingerbread in Little Pans (see pg. 75)

Almond Cheesecakes Another Way

Six ounces of almonds, blanch'd and beat with rose-water; six ounces of butter beat to cream; half a pound of fine sugar; six eggs well beat, and a little mace. Bake these in little tins, in cold butter paste.

—*English Housewifery*,
Elizabeth Moxon, p. 12 (1775)

Almond Cheesecakes

1½ sticks (12 tablespoons) butter + additional butter for greasing the tins

¾ cup almonds, blanched and ground to flour or 5 tablespoons (3 ounces) blanched almond flour

1 cup fine sugar

1 tablespoon rose water

6 medium eggs

½ teaspoon ground mace

1. Make a pie crust to line 2-inch muffin tins. Butter the tins heavily before lining with the pie crust.
2. Cream 1½ sticks of butter.
3. In a separate bowl, beat the eggs well.
4. Add the almond flour, sugar, rose water, and mace to the eggs.
5. Add in the butter.
6. Bake at 350°F for 25 minutes. Then turn off the oven, leaving the cheesecakes in for an additional 8–10 minutes—just until the top is fawn-colored.

A Butter Drop

Four yolks, two whites, one pound flour, a quarter of a pound butter, one pound sugar, two spoons rose water, a little mace, baked in tin pans.

—*American Cookery*,
Amelia Simmons, p. 38 (1796)

Butter Drops

¼ pound (1 stick) butter

2 cups sugar

4 egg yolks

2 egg whites

2 cups flour

2 tablespoons rose water

¼–½ heaping ground teaspoon mace

1. Cream butter and sugar until light and fluffy.

2. Add egg yolks and whites, and just combine—do not overbeat.

3. Add flour, and just combine—do not overbeat.

4. Add rose water and mace. Gently beat until just combined.

5. Spoon into 2½-inch muffin tins. Fill about two-thirds full.

6. Bake at 350°F for 22–24 minutes. If muffins are browning too much, cover with foil after 15–18 minutes.

7. Turn off the oven. Keeping the oven door closed, leave the muffins in for another 3–5 minutes.

Common Biscuits

BEAT eight eggs well up together, and mix with them a pound of sifted sugar with the rind of a lemon grated. Whisk it about till it looks light, and then put in a pound of flour, with a little rose-water. Sugar them over, and bake them in tins, or on papers.

—The Housekeeper's Instructor or,
Universal Family Cook, W.A.
Henderson, p. 218 (14th edition 1807)

Common Biscuits

This recipe can be made three ways: small muffins, small cakes (cookies), or a cake.
This is a half recipe.

4 medium eggs
1 cup sugar
1 lemon rind, grated
1 cup flour
¼–½ teaspoon rose water (to taste)
1 tablespoon sugar (to sprinkle on top to taste)

1. Preheat the oven to 325°F.
2. Beat the eggs well; then add the sugar and lemon rind.
3. Whisk until the mixture looks light. Then add the flour and rose water, and mix.
4. *Now the fun part!*
   - For muffins, use a 2-inch muffin pan; fill each cavity two-thirds full. Bake at 325°F for 10–12 minutes. Turn off oven, and leave the pan in for another 5–7 minutes until done. Do not let them brown.
   - For small cakes, drop batter on baking sheets by tablespoons. Bake at 325°F for 12 minutes.
   - For a cake, use a springform pan, filling it halfway (I used a 4½-inch springform pan). Bake at 325°F for 20–22 minutes.

Little Currant and Seed Cakes

Take two pounds of fine flour, one pound and a half of butter, the yolks of five or six eggs, one pound and a half of sugar, six spoonfuls of rose-water, nine spoonfuls of sack, three spoonfuls of carraway seeds, two nutmegs, and one pound of currants; beat the butter with your hand till it is very thin, dry your flour well, put in your carraway seeds and nutmegs finely grated, afterwards put them all into your batter, with your eggs, sack, and rose-water, mingle them well together, put in your currants, let your oven be pretty hot, and as soon as they are colored they will be enough.

—*The Compleat Confectioner; or,*
the Whole Art of Confectionary Made Plain
and Easy. Hannah Glasse, p. 81 (1753)

Currant and Seed Cakes

This half recipe yields approximately 24 2-inch muffins or 24–36 small cakes.

1½ cups butter

2 cups flour

1½ tablespoons caraway seed

1 tablespoon nutmeg

2–3 egg yolks (1 large, 1 medium yolk or 3 medium yolks)

1½ cups sugar

4½–5 tablespoons sack

3 tablespoons rose water

1 cup currants

1. Preheat the oven at 400°F.
2. Beat the butter until it is pale and thin.
3. In a separate bowl, mix the flour, caraway seeds, and nutmeg together.
4. Add the egg yolks, sack, and rose water to the butter; mix just to combine.
5. Add flour mixture to the butter batter, and stir to combine.
6. Mix in the currants.
7. *Two ways to bake!*
   - For muffins, use a 2-inch muffin pan; fill the cavities two-thirds full. Bake for 12–14 minutes or just until turning golden.
   - For small cakes, drop by tablespoons onto parchment-lined baking sheets. Bake at 400°F for 4–6 minutes.

To Make Drop Biscuits

BEAT the yolks of ten eggs, and the whites of six, with one spoonful of rose water, half an hour, then put in ten ounces of loaf sugar beat and sifted, whisk them well for half an hour, then add one ounce of carraway seeds crushed a little, and six ounces of fine flour, whisk in your flour gently, drop them on wafer papers, and bake them in a moderate oven.

—*The Experienced English Housekeeper*,
Elizabeth Raffald, p. 276 (1776)

Drop Biscuits

This half recipe yields about 24 small cakes.

5 medium egg yolks
3 medium egg whites
2 teaspoons rose water
⅝ cup sugar, sifted
1 teaspoon slightly crushed caraway seeds
⅞ cup flour

1. Preheat oven to 300°F.
2. Beat the egg yolks and egg whites with the rose water very well (should be frothy).
3. Add the sugar, and whisk it in very well.
4. Add the caraway seeds, and gently whisk in the flour.
5. Drop batter by tablespoons onto parchment paper–lined baking sheet, and bake for 12–15 minutes. They are done when just turning fawn-colored.

Soft Gingerbread to Be Baked in Pans

Rub three pounds of sugar, two pounds of butter, into four pounds of flour, add 20 eggs, 4 ounces ginger, 4 spoons rose water, bake 15 minutes.

—American Cookery,
Amelia Simmons, p. 36 (1796)

Gingerbread in Little Pans

1 pound (4 sticks) butter

3 cups sugar

4 cups flour

10 eggs

4 tablespoons ground ginger

¾–1 cup rose water

1. Cream butter until light.
2. Mix in the sugar and flour.
3. Add the eggs, ginger, and rose water.
4. Spoon batter into little pans (I used 12–cavity mini-bundt pans).
5. Bake at 325°F for 35–40 minutes. Leaving the oven door closed, turn off the oven, and let bake for another 5–8 minutes. They are done when a toothpick comes out with a small, soft crumb.

Heart Cakes
(Rosewater-Current Cakes)

Beat one pound of butter to a cream with some rosewater one pound flour dried one pound sifted sugar 12 eggs. Beat all together. Add a few currants washed and dried. Butter some small pans heart shaped pour mixture grate sugar over them. They are soon baked in a Dutch oven.

—Her Receipts 1796, Confections, Savouries and Drams, Fanny Pierson Crane, p. 21

Rose Water-Currant Cakes

1 cup sugar

1 cup butter

3 eggs

1 teaspoon rose water

2¾ cups flour

½ cup currants

1. Preheat oven to 375°F.
2. Cream the sugar and butter until light and fluffy.
3. Add the eggs, one at a time, beating well after each addition.
4. Stir in the rose water, then add the flour and currants.
5. Drop batter by tablespoons onto a baking sheet, roll into balls, and press down gently.
6. Bake for 12–15 minutes or until the edges are lightly browned.

To make little Almond Cakes

Take a pound of sugar and eight eggs, beat them well an hour, then put them into a pound of flour, beat them together, blanch a quarter of a pound of almonds, and beat them with rose-water to keep 'em from oiling, mix all together, butter your tins, and bake them half an hour.

Half an hour is rather too long for them to stand in the oven.

—*English Housewifery*,
Elizabeth Moxon, p. 159 (349), (1775)

Little Almond Cakes

5 egg yolks
1 cup sugar
1 tablespoon rose water
1 cup flour
¼ teaspoon salt
4 tablespoons blanched almond flour

1. Separate eggs.
2. Beat egg yolks until thick and lemon-colored.
3. Gradually add sugar and rose water, beating well.
4. In a separate bowl, sift flour with salt.
5. Gradually stir flour, then almonds, into the batter.
6. Fill very well-buttered muffin tins two-thirds full.
7. Bake in a 350°F oven about 12–15 minutes or until the tops are very light brown.*
8. Cool in pan on a wire rack for 10 minutes. To remove cakes, gently twist until they release.

*Even Elizabeth Moxon thought that a half hour is too long to leave the cakes in the oven. She corrected her own recipe in print!

Little Queen's Cakes

Take two pounds of fine flour, a pound and half of butter, the yolks of six eggs, one pound and a half of sugar, six spoonfuls of rose-water, nine spoonfuls of sack, two nutmegs, and two pounds of currants, beat your butter with your hand till it is very thin, dry your flour very well, put in your sugar and nutmegs finely grated, and put them all into your batter, with your eggs, sack, and rose-water mingle them well together, put in your currants, let your oven be moderately hot, and they will be baked in a quarter of an hour; take care your currants be nicely washed and cleaned.

—The Compleat Confectioner;
or the Whole Art of Confectionary Made
Plain and Easy, Hannah Glasse, p. 83 (1742)

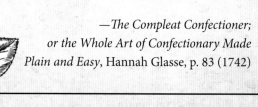

Little Queen's Cakes

This half recipe yields 24–36 little 2-inch muffins.

3 cups flour
1½ cups (3 sticks) butter
2⅛ cups sugar
1 tablespoon nutmeg
3 medium egg yolks
4–5 tablespoons sack (sherry)
3 tablespoons rose water
2 cups currants

1. Beat the butter until it is pale and very soft.
2. Add the sugar and nutmeg, and mix.
3. Put the egg yolks, flour, sack, and rose water into the batter, and mix until blended.
4. Add the currants, and stir them in.
5. Put the batter into small 2-inch muffin tins.
6. Bake at 325°F for 20–26 minutes or until a toothpick comes out clean.

Macaroons

Take a pound of blanched almonds and beat them, put some rose-water in while beating; (they must not be beaten too small) mix them with the whites of five eggs, a pound of sugar finely beaten and sifted, and a handful of flour, mix all these very well together, lay them on wafers, and bake them in a very temperate oven, (it must not be so hot as for manchet) then they are fit for use.

—*English Housewifery*, Elizabeth Moxon,
p. 112 (240), (1775)

Rose Macaroons

2½ cups blanched almond flour
1–1½ tablespoons rose water
5 egg whites
3½ cups sugar, sifted
handful of flour (approx. ½ cup)

1. Beat the blanched almond flour with the rose water.
2. Mix in the egg whites, sugar, and handful of flour. Beat well.
3. Drop the batter by tablespoons onto parchment paper–lined baking sheet, and bake at 225°F for about 25–30 minutes or until just a touch of color appears.

To Make Portugal Cakes

Mix into a Pound of fine Flour, a Pound of Loaf Sugar beat and sifted, then rub into it a Pound of pure sweet Butter, till it is thick like grated white Bread, then put to it two Spoonfuls of Rose water, two of Sack, ten Eggs, whip them very well with a Whisk, then mix into it eight Ounces of Currants, mix'd all well together; butter the Tin-pans, fill them but half full, and bake them; if made without Currants they'll keep half a Year; add a Pound of Almonds blanch'd, and beat with Rose-water as above, and leave out the Flour. These are another Sort and better.

—*The Art of Cookery Made Plain and Easy,* Hannah Glasse, p. 288 (1753)

Portugal Cakes

This is a half recipe.

1⅔ cups flour
1⅔ cups sugar, sifted
1 cup butter
1 tablespoon rose water
1 tablespoon sack
5 eggs
4 ounces currants

1. Combine the flour and sifted sugar.
2. Mix in the butter until you have a crumbly mixture much like a streusel topping.
3. To the mixture, add the rose water, sack, and eggs. Whip it well with a whisk.
4. Add the currants, and mix well.
5. Butter well the cavities of a 2-inch muffin tin and fill them each halfway.
6. Bake at 325°F for 26–28 minutes.

Rout Drop Cakes

Mix two pounds of flour, one ditto butter, one ditto sugar, one ditto currants, clean and dry; then wet into a stiff paste, with two eggs, a large spoon of orange flower-water, ditto rose-water, ditto sweet wine, ditto brandy, drop on a tin-plate floured: a very short time bakes them.

—*Domestic Cookery for Private Families*,
Maria Rundell, p. 234 (1808)

Rout Drop Cakes

1 cup flour

½ cup unsalted butter, softened

½ cup caster sugar

1 egg

1 teaspoon orange-flower water or orange juice

1 teaspoon rose water

1½ teaspoons sweet white wine

1½ teaspoons brandy

¼ cup currants

pinch of salt

granulated sugar for topping

1. Grease a baking sheet.
2. Sift the flour and salt into a bowl. Work in the butter and sugar until well mixed.
3. In a small bowl, beat the egg until liquid. Add the orange-flower water (or orange juice), rose water, wine, and brandy. Mix well.
4. Slowly mix the egg mixture into the flour mixture to get a smooth dough. Add the currants.
5. Place small teaspoons of batter (a ball of batter approx. ¾" in diameter) on the greased baking sheet. Sprinkle the granulated sugar on top.
6. Bake at 325°F for 15–18 minutes. Do not overbake.
7. Cool on a wire rack.

Shrewsbury Cakes

TAKE two pounds of flour, a pound of sugar finely searched, mix them together (take out a quarter of a pound to roll them in) take four eggs beat, four spoonfuls of cream, and two spoonfuls of rose-water; beat them well together, and mix them with the flour into a paste, roll them into thin cakes, and bake them in a quick oven.

—*The Art of Cookery Made Plain and Easy*, Hannah Glasse, p. 276 (1774)

Shrewsbury Cakes

2 cups sugar

2 cups butter

1 teaspoon nutmeg, grated

3 eggs, beaten

¼ cup sherry

¼ cup rose water

4 cups flour, sifted

1. Cream sugar with butter until very fluffy. Add the nutmeg and salt.
2. In a separate bowl, combine the well-beaten eggs with the sherry and rose water. Add to the butter-and-sugar mixture.
3. Gradually mix in the sifted flour and blend well.
4. On a lightly floured board, roll the dough very thin, to about ¼-inch thickness.
5. Cut the dough with a 4-inch cookie cutter. Prick each with a fork.
6. Bake in a slow oven at 300°F until golden brown.

Soft Cakes in Little Pans

One and half pound sugar, half pound butter, rubbed into two pounds flour, add one glass wine, one do. rose water, 18 eggs and a nutmeg.

—*American Cookery*,
Amelia Simmons, p. 37 (1796)

Soft Cakes in Little Pans

This is a half recipe.

1½ cups sugar

¼ pound (1 stick) butter

2 cups flour

1 glass wine (just over ⅓ cup of a white dessert wine)

1 glass (⅓–½ cup) rose water

9 medium eggs

1 nutmeg, grated

1. Combine sugar and butter. Beat until very light. Add flour.
2. Add wine, rose water, eggs, and nutmeg.
3. Bake at 325°F for 24–26 minutes (if using 2-inch muffin pan).
4. Without opening the door, turn off the oven, and leave the little cakes in for 8–10 minutes more or until a toothpick comes out clean.

How to Make Sugar Biscuits a Cheap Way

Take one pound of fine flour, one pound of powder sugar, a few almonds blanched and pounded, mix these with six spoonfuls of rose water, and the yolk and whites of eight eggs that are beat a full hour; when well mixed, put it into small tin pans of various fashions, and bake them only with the heat of the oven after the batch is drawn, and stop the oven very close.

—*The Complete Confectioner; or, the Whole Art of Confectionary Made Plain and Easy,* Hannah Glasse, p. 74 (1742)

Sugar Biscuits

This is a half recipe.

4 medium egg whites
4 medium egg yolks
1 cup flour
1 cup sugar
¼ cup almond flour
2¼ tablespoons rose water

1. Beat the egg whites to soft peaks. In another bowl, beat the yolks smooth.
2. Mix the flour, sugar, almond flour, and rose water together.
3. Combine everything, and mix well.
4. Put into small molds, and bake at 325°F for 18–20 minutes. They are done when a toothpick comes out with a soft crumb. Do not overbake.

Sugar Cakes

Take ½ pound of fine Sugar, Sierced, and as much flour, two eggs beaten with a little Rose water, and a piece of Butter about the Bigness of an Egg, work them well together till they be a Smooth paste, then Roll them and Cut them with Glasses. Lay them on plates Rubbed with Butter, and Bake them in an Oven just Warm.

—*The Art of Cookery Plain and Easy,*
Hannah Glasse (Dublin 1758)

Sugar Cakes

1 cup granulated sugar
1 cup all-purpose flour
2 medium eggs
2 teaspoons rose water
3 tablespoons salted butter, divided

1. Mix the sugar and flour.
2. In a separate bowl, beat the eggs with the rose water. Add this mixture plus 2 tablespoons of butter to the sugar and flour mixture.
3. Mix thoroughly with your hands, then roll out the dough, and cut out circles with a wine glass.
4. Lightly grease two baking sheets with remaining tablespoon of butter. Place the circles on the sheets.
5. Bake at 200°F for 50 minutes or until the edge of the cakes just start turning a fawn color.

Begger's Pudding
(see pg. 149)

Pies and Tarts

Pies and tarts have pastry crusts and often pudding, or cream, fillings. A busy household might not have enough room to accommodate breads, cakes, and pies in the same oven. It was not uncommon for pies and tarts to be cooked at a public bake house (marked with the owner's initials or a design on the top), then brought back home while they were still cooling off.

Apple Pudding Tart
99

Custard Tart
105

Apple Tansy
101

Orange Pudding
107

Cream Tart in the Italian Fashion
103

Set Custard
109

Apple Pudding

One pound apple sifted, one pound sugar, 9 eggs, one quarter of a pound butter, one quart sweet cream, one gill rose-water, a cinnamon, a green lemon peal grated (if sweet apples) add the juice of half a lemon, put on paste No. 7.* Currants, raisins and citron some add, but good without them.

*No. 7 pie crust (A Paste for Sweet Meats)

Rub one third of a pound of butter, and one pound of lard into two pound flour, wet with four whites well beaten; water q: s: to make a paste, roll in the residue of shortning in ten or twelve rollings- bake quick

—*American Cookery,*
Amelia Simmons, p. 27 (1796)

Apple Pudding Tart

1 pound apples

2 cups sugar

9 eggs

½ pound (2 sticks) butter (softened)

1 quart sweet cream

½ cup (4 ounces) rose water

1 tablespoon cinnamon

1 lemon peel, grated

juice of ½ lemon

1. In a saucepan, steam apples in 2 cups water. When soft and skins split open, remove from heat.
2. Let cool a bit, then remove the meat from the apple and either mash or strain it. Remove all skin and core.
3. In a mixer, place your sugar, butter, eggs, sweet cream, rose water, cinnamon, lemon peel, and lemon juice. Combine.
4. Add mashed apples to mixture and blend.
5. Pour into 2 deep pie shells and bake at 350°F for 1½ hours. Check at 30 minutes to see if your pie shell is browning too fast; if so, place a foil tent over the pies.

Apple Tansy

Take three Pippins, slice them round in thin Slices, and fry them with Butter; then beat four Eggs with six Spoonfuls of Cream, a little Rose-Water, Nutmeg and Sugar; stir them together, and pour it over the Apples, let it fry a little and then turn it with a pye-plate; Garnish with Lemon and Sugar strewed over it.

—The Compleat Housewife:
or Accomplished Gentlewoman's
Companion, Eliza Smith, p. 150 (1728)

Apple Tansy

2–3 tart apples, such as Macintosh or Granny
    Smith
2 tablespoons butter
4 eggs
½ cup heavy cream

½ teaspoon nutmeg, freshly grated
¼ cup rose water
3 tablespoons sugar
¼ fresh lemon
2 teaspoons powdered sugar

1. Peel and core the apples. Slice into ¼-inch-thick rings.
2. In a large nonstick skillet, melt the butter on medium heat. Cook and stir the apples in the butter until slightly browned on both sides (approx. 12–15 minutes). Spread the apples evenly over the bottom of the skillet.
3. While the apples are cooking, mix the eggs, cream, nutmeg, and rose water, gradually adding the sugar. Whip until frothy, about 1–2 minutes.
4. Pour the egg mixture over the cooked apples while in the skillet on medium heat. Rotate the pan just enough to distribute the mixture evenly. Cook covered for 5 minutes. Reduce the heat to low, and continue to cook covered until there is no visible egg liquid remaining (about 6–7 minutes). Do not burn.
5. Shake the skillet to loosen the tansy, and turn upside down (apple side up). Drizzle lemon and powdered sugar on top.

To Make a Cream Tart in the Italian Fashion to Eat Cold

Take twenty yolks of eggs, and two quarts of cream, strain it with a little salt, saffron, rose-water, juice of orange, a little white-wine, and a pound of fine sugar, then bake it in a deep dish with some fine cinnamon, and some candied pistachios stuck on it, and when it is baked, white muskedines.

Thus you may do with the whites of the eggs, and put in no spices.

—*The Accomplisht Cook, or,*
The Whole Art and Mystery of Cookery,
Fitted for All Degrees and Qualities,
Robert May, p. 286 (1685)

Cream Tart in the Italian Fashion

10 medium egg yolks

1 quart cream

2–3 small threads of saffron

1 tablespoon white wine

1 tablespoon rose water

⅛ cup orange juice

1⅔ cups sugar

one pie shell

cinnamon (to sprinkle on top)

1. Cover a large bowl with cheesecloth. Using a spatula, strain the egg yolks and cream through the cheesecloth.
2. Remove the cheesecloth. Add the white wine, rose water, salt, orange juice, and sugar. Combine.
3. Line a deep 9½-inch or 10-inch pie pan with the pie shell and partially bake for 6 minutes at 375°F.
4. Pour the mixture into the pie shell. Sprinkle the cinnamon on top, and bake at 350°F for approximately 1 hour 5 minutes.
5. Cover the pie, and bake for another 10–15 minutes.

Custard Tart

To three pints of Cream, put a little whole Mace, Cinnamon and Nutmeg; make it boil a little, then take it off, and beat fifteen Eggs very well, leaving out nine of the Whites; when beaten, put to them a Glas of Sack, and two Spoonfuls of Rose Water; put it to the Cream scalding hot, then strain it, and it is fit; harden the Custard Crust in the Oven before you fill them. To all Milk, put sixteen Eggs; to two Quarts, leave out five Whites.

—*The Housekeeper's Pocket-book*,
Mrs. Sarah Harrison, pp. 56-57 (1760)

Custard Tart

This half recipe yields one 9-inch pie.

1 prebaked pie crust
1½ pints cream
5–6 pieces whole mace
1 tablespoon cinnamon
1 teaspoon nutmeg

3 medium whole eggs
3 medium and 1 large egg yolk (just yolks, no whites)
¼ cup sack (sherry)
2 tablespoons rose water

1. In a heavy saucepan, heat the cream, mace, cinnamon, and nutmeg until it just begins to boil.
2. Remove the saucepan from the heat.
3. In a bowl, beat the eggs and egg yolks very well. Once beaten, add the sack and rose water.
4. Add the egg mixture to the cream mixture, and stir it gently.
5. Strain the mixture, and gently pour it into the prebaked pie shell.
6. Bake at 350°F for approximately 1 hour. If the custard starts to brown, cover with tin foil, and continue to bake.

To Make a Second Sort of Orange Pudding

You must take sixteen Yolks of Eggs, beat them fine, mix them with half a Pound of fresh Butter melted, and half a Pound of white Sugar, a little Rose-water and a little Nutmeg. Cut the Peel of a fine large Seville Orange so thin as that none of the White appears, beat it fine in a Mortar, till it is like a Paste, and by degrees mix in the above Ingredients all together, then lay a Puff paste all over the Dish, pour in the ingredients, and bake it.

—*The Art of Cookery Made Plain and Easy,* Hannah Glasse, p. 228 (1753)

Orange Pudding

This half recipe yields one 9-inch tart.

Seville or any available orange peel (beat fine)
8 medium egg yolks
½ cup butter, melted
½ cup sugar

1 teaspoon rose water
½ teaspoon nutmeg
puff paste for tart pan

1. Using a mortar and pestle, beat the orange peel into a paste.
2. In a bowl, beat the egg yolks well. Add the melted butter, sugar, rose water, and nutmeg.
3. By degrees, add the paste-like orange peel.
4. Mix all until blended.
5. Lay your puff pastry into the pie pan, and pour the ingredients into it.
6. Bake at 350°F for about 15 minutes, then turn down the oven to 300°F. If it starts to brown, cover with a foil tent.
7. Continue baking at 300°F for an additional 55–60 minutes.
8. Turn your oven off, leaving the door closed, and let the tart sit for another 10 minutes before taking it out of the oven.

Set Custards

Set to boil over the Fire a Quart of Cream, with some broad Mace; when it's boiled set it to be cold, then take six Eggs with half the Whites, beat them very well, and put in a Spoonful of Orange-flower-water, or Rosewater, and put in a Pound of Sugar; harden the Crust in the Oven, stuff the corners with brown Paper, and prick the Bottoms with a small Pin to prevent them rising in Blisters, when you set them and fill them, and when they are enough set them by for Use.

—*The Art of Cookery Made Plain and Easy*, Hannah Glasse, p. 368, (1753)

Set Custard

Make a pie crust or two depending on the size you wish.

1 quart cream
5–8 pieces of broad mace
6 egg yolks
3 egg whites
2 tablespoons rose-water
1 cup sugar (more if to taste)

1. In a double boiler or heavy saucepan, bring the cream and mace to barely a boil. Stir it constantly—do not allow it to come to a rolling boil.
2. Take it off the flame, and set it aside to cool.
3. Beat the egg yolks and egg whites very well. Add the rose-water and sugar, and beat until combined.
4. Gently pour the egg mixture into your pie shell.
5. Bake at 325°F for approximately 55 minutes. Watch that your custard does not burn. If browning too fast, cover tart with foil, and continue baking.
6. Turn off oven, leaving the door closed, and let tart stand in the heated oven for another 5–8 minutes.

French Flummery
(see pg. 127)

Creams, Custards, and Puddings

Boiled, baked, or cooked, creams, custards, and puddings are all cream-based recipes that come in almost infinite varieties. They were served by the poorest cooks as well as the most extravagant households. The recipes ranged from a few simple ingredients to a complex selection of flavors, which could include fruits, nuts, and spices.

Snow and Cream (see pg. 143)

Almond Custard

Take a quarter of a pound of almonds, blanch and beat them very fine, and then put them into a pint of cream, with two spoonfuls of rose water. Sweeten it to your palate; beat up the yolks of four eggs, very fine, and put them in. Stir all together one way over the fire, till it is thick, and then pour it into cups.

—*The Whole Art of Confectionary,*
A Person, London, p. 21

Almond Custard

2 cups heavy cream

1 stick cinnamon

3 ounces blanched almonds, ground

1 teaspoon rose water

½ cup sugar

1 egg

5 egg yolks

2 tablespoons brandy

1. Bring cream and cinnamon stick to a boil. Remove cinnamon.
2. Add almonds, rose water, and sugar.
3. In a separate pan, beat egg and yolks. Place over low heat. Add hot cream mixture, stirring continuously.
4. Continue cooking and stirring until the custard coats a spoon. Stir in brandy.
5. Pour into small pots or glass dishes. Chill.

To Make Apple Cream

Take half a dozen large apples (codlings or any other apples that will be soft) and coddle them; when they are cold take out the pulp; then take the whites of four or five eggs, (leaving out the strains) three quarters of pound of double refined sugar beat and sifted, a spoonful or two of rose-water and grate in a little lemon-peel, so beat all together for an hour, whilst it be white, then lay it on a china dish, so serve it up.

—English Housewifery,
Elizabeth Moxon, p. 117 (1775)

Apple Cream

6 large apples (baking variety)
4–5 egg whites (remove strains, which are the white on yolks)
½ cup caster sugar (to taste)
1–2 tablespoons rose water
½–¾ teaspoon grated lemon peel

1. Place the apples in a saucepan with a lid. Add ½ to ¾ inches water, and place the lid on the pan.
2. Steam the apples until soft.
3. Take the apples off the heat, drain off the water, and allow the apples to cool completely.
4. When cold, remove all the apple pulp. Do not use the core, seeds, skin, or stem.
5. Combine the egg whites, sugar, rose water, and lemon peel with the apple pulp. and beat until it becomes white and airy.
6. Place the apple cream in a china bowl.
7. Allow this mixture to sit for at least 1 hour before serving.

Baked Custard

One Pint of Cream, boil with Mace and Cinnamon, when cold take four Eggs, two Whites left out, a little Rose and Orange-flower-Water and Sack, Nutmeg and Sugar to your Palate, mix them well together, and bake them in China-cups.

—*The Art of Cookery Made Plain and Easy*, Hannah Glasse, p. 284 (1762)

Baked Custard

2 cups heavy cream

½ teaspoon ground mace

1 tablespoon + ¾ teaspoon ground cinnamon

1 teaspoon rose water

1¼ teaspoons orange-flower water

4 tablespoons dry sherry

2 eggs

2 egg yolks

½ cup sugar

1. Preheat oven to 300°F.
2. In a heavy saucepan, bring the cream, mace, and cinnamon to almost boiling (200°F) on medium heat, stirring continuously so that no skin forms. Cook until this mixture thickens enough to coat a wooden spoon (approx. 5 minutes). Remove from heat, and set aside to cool.
3. In a separate bowl, combine the rose water, orange-flower water, and sherry. Stir into the cooled cream mixture, and set it aside.
4. In a bowl, beat the eggs and yolks together.
5. Gradually beat the egg mixture and the sugar into the cream mixture.
6. Pour the custard into 6-ounce cups or ramekins. Place the cups in a baking dish, and place it in the oven. Pour water into the baking dish until it is halfway up the sides of the cups or ramekins.
7. Bake about 25–30 minutes until a wooden toothpick inserted into the center comes out clean. Let cool, then refrigerate.

Berry/Currant Fool

Place your currans and raspberries in a stone bason; put into a kettle filled to halfe with water, boil it gently til the berries soften, stirring; take the bason from the fire and let stand til cool; when cold sweeten it to your taste; slowly add the cream stirring all the time; strain it, and force it through your strainer; draw it up and serve.

—*The Compleat Practical Cook*,
Charles Carter (London, 1730)

Berry Fool

1 (16-ounce) bag mixed frozen berries
2 tablespoons caster sugar
½ teaspoon rose water (or more, to taste)
1 pint heavy whipping cream

1. Put the frozen berries and sugar in a pan. Heat gently until just boiling and the fruit juices are released. Remove from the heat.
2. Transfer the mixture to a bowl, and let it cool. Then place in the refrigerator for 1–2 hours.
3. When the fruit is chilled, strain it through a fine sieve, reserving the juice.
4. Gently crush the fruit with a fork, leaving some fruit whole. Add the rose water, and mix thoroughly.
5. In a separate bowl, whisk the cream until it starts to thicken. When the cream develops soft peaks, stir in the fruit, and mix gently to combine.
6. Mixture may be put in a large glass bowl or individual glasses to serve. Drizzle the reserved fruit juices over the cream mixture. You may decorate with candied rose petals.

Carrot Pudding

To make a carrett pudding Greate two penny loaves of bread and an equall Quantity of carretts 1 Nutmeg ½ a pound of melted butter 4 or 5 spoonfulls of Rose Water and a little salt. Mingle these well together put all onto a pann that is buttered lett it bake 2 hours then turn it out. The properest sauce is Roase water and Sugar.

—Margaretta Acworth's Georgian Cookery Book (private journal)

A coffee cup full of boiled and strained carrots, 5 eggs, sugar and butter of each 2 oz. cinnamon and rose water to your taste, baked in a deep dish without paste, 1 hour.

—American Cookery, Amelia Simmons, p. 34 (1796, second edition)

Carrot Pudding

3 cups breadcrumbs

2 cups grated carrots

⅝ cup sugar

1 nutmeg, grated

2 cups milk or milk and cream mixed

¼ cup butter (optional)

2 large eggs + 1 large egg yolk, lightly beaten

1 tablespoon rose water (or more, to taste)

1. Grate the bread and carrot together in a bowl or food processor.
2. Stir in the sugar and nutmeg.
3. Warm the milk to approximately 98°F, melting the butter in it if you desire.
4. In a separate bowl, pour the warmed milk over the lightly beaten eggs, stirring gently; add the rose water. Then pour this mixture over the dry ingredients.
5. Mix well, and spoon the finished mixture into a 9-inch cake tin or ring mold.
6. Bake at 325°F for 2 hours.
7. Test it with a toothpick to check that it is firm.
8. Turn out onto a warm plate, and serve immediately, with a little sugar melted in some rose water or with cream.

To Make a Fine Cream

Take a Pint of Cream, sweeten it to your Palate, grate a little Nutmeg, put in a Spoonful of Orange-flower Water or Rose-water, and two Spoonfuls of Sack, beat up four Eggs, but two Whites; stir all together one Way over the Fire till it is thick, have Cups ready and pour in.

—*The Art of Cookery, Made Plain and Easy,*
Hannah Glasse, p. 296 (1753)

Fine Cream

1 pint heavy cream
2–4 tablespoons sugar (to taste)
¼ teaspoon nutmeg
1 tablespoon orange-flower water
1 tablespoon rose water
2 tablespoons sack
4 medium egg yolks
2 medium egg whites

1. Pour cream into a heavy saucepan or double boiler. Add sugar.
2. Add the nutmeg, orange-flower water, rose water, and sack.
3. In a bowl, beat the egg yolks and whites until well combined. Add to cream mixture.
4. Stir mixture constantly until it is thick.
5. Remove from heat, cool slightly, and pour into cups.

French Flummery

BEAT half an ounce of isinglass fine, put to it a quart of cream, and mix them well together. Let it boil softly over a slow fire for a quarter of an hour, and keep stirring it all the time. Then take it off, sweeten it to your taste, and put in a spoonful of rose-water, and another of orange-flower-water. Strain it, and pour it into a glass or bason, or whatever else you please, and when cold, turn it out.

—The London Art of Cookery,
John Farley, p. 242 (1783)

French Flummery

1 quart cream
1 tablespoon unflavored gelatin
¼–½ cup sugar
1 tablespoon rose water (to taste)
1 tablespoon orange-flower water

1. Put the cream and gelatin in a saucepan. Stir over medium heat. Let boil very gently for 15 minutes, but continue stirring the entire time.
2. Remove from the heat.
3. Stir in the sugar, water, and orange-flower water.
4. Pour the mixture into glasses or a small mold, and allow to cool.
5. Refrigerate to cool further.
6. If in a glass basin or mold, turn out onto a plate to serve.

Portugal Cream

Break a doz. Eggs or more according to the size of Your Tin.
Beat them very well, and Strain them into Your Stew pan.
put a little Rose or Orange water to them, with Half a pint of
Cream. Sweeten to your Taste, Set it on the Fire, and Stirr it
till it Boils and grows thick. then pour it into Your Tin. when
Cold, Turn it upon what you please.

—(from an anonymous manuscript ca.
1758 in the collection of Vincent DiMarco)
DiMarco, Vincent, *Egg Pies, Moss Cakes,
and Pigeons Like Puffins, Eighteenth-
Century British Cookery from Manuscript
Sources*, (iUniverse, Inc., p. 57, 2007)

Portugal Cream

12 eggs
1 tablespoon rose water
¼ cup sugar

1. Break the eggs into a large bowl and beat until light and frothy.
2. Strain the eggs through cheesecloth into another bowl.
3. Add the rose water and sugar and beat until very well blended and frothy.
4. Place the mixture in a double boiler; stir constantly until it boils and thickens.
5. Allow the mixture to cool, then put it into a serving dish or glasses.

Pare Plumb Cream

Take the pareplumbs & boyle th(e)m tender then pill of all the skins & take out all the stones & mash the pulp altogether, th(e)n put three spoonfull of Rose water and a pint of fare water and the yelks and whites of six Eggs well beaten then sweeten it with some fine sugger and sett it one the fire keeping it continually stirring one way till it thickens like cream then take it off and when cold dish it up.

—*Recipes from the Great Houses,* p. 95, Michael Barry, (1996) from the Twisden Family, Bradbourne Park, 1675–1750

Pare Plum Cream

2 pounds greengage plums, cut in half

1 cup water

1 teaspoon rose water

½–¾ cup (4–6 ounces) caster sugar

6 medium eggs

1. In a heavy saucepan, place the plums in the water. Simmer until soft and the pits float free.
2. Remove the pits and the skins.
3. In a blender, puree the plums.
4. In a double boiler, or heavy saucepan, place the pureed plums, rose water, and sugar. Stir until the sugar is completely dissolved.
5. In a separate bowl, beat the eggs and gently add to the plum mixture, stirring continuously until the mixture thickens to a thinner custard-like texture.
6. Remove the mixture from the heat, and allow it to cool. It will thicken.
7. Place the cooled mixture into individual cups or ramekins, and refrigerate.

Raspberry Cream

Take half a pound of preserved raspberries, wet, and bruise them, and boil them gently up in a quart of cream; put in a blade of mace; season them with fine sugar, orange-flower or rose water; strain it, and force it through your strainer, and then draw it up with the yolks of three eggs, and put it in basins or glasses.

—Charles Carter, Cook to the Duke
of Argyll, the Earl of Pontefract and
Lord Cornwallis (Private journal, 1730)

Raspberry Cream

1½ cups (½ pound) fresh raspberries (or 10-ounce packet frozen raspberries)
1 pint heavy single cream
4 egg yolks
½ cup (4 ounces) sugar
½ teaspoon ground mace
4 tablespoons rose water (or orange-flower water)

1. Rub the raspberries through a fine sieve, and add enough cream to make 2½ cups (1 pint).
2. In a saucepan, on medium setting, heat the cream and raspberry purée to just below boiling point.
3. Beat together the egg yolks, sugar, mace, and rose water (or orange-flower water).
4. Pour the cream and raspberry mixture into the egg mixture in a thin stream, and beat until smooth.
5. Cook in the top of a double boiler, over simmering water, until it is thick enough to coat a spoon.
6. Pour into a serving bowl, and chill.

Rice Cream

Mix three Spoonfuls of the Flour of Rice, as much Sugar, the Yolks of two Eggs, two Spoonfuls of Sack, or Rose, or Orange-flower-water, all well together, and put them to a Pint of Cream; stir it over the Fire, till it is thick, then pour it into China Dishes. It may be glaz'd as your Fancy leads you.

—*The New Art of Cookery Made Plain and Easy*, Hannah Glasse, p. 395 (1753)

Rice Cream

3 tablespoons rice flour

3 tablespoons sugar

2 egg yolks

2–3 tablespoons rose water or orange-flower water or sack (to taste)

1 pint cream

1. Mix rice flour, sugar, egg yolks, and rose water (or orange-flower water or sack).
2. Add to a pint of cream, and stir in heavy pan over medium heat until thick.
3. Pour into porcelain dishes that can handle heat.

Rice Custards

Take a Quart of Cream, and boil it with a Blade of Mace; then put to it boiled Rice, well beaten with your Cream; put them together, and stir them well all the while it boils on the Fire; and when it's enough take it off, and sweeten it to your Taste, and put in a little Rose water; let them be cold, then serve them.

—The Art of Cookery Plain and Easy,
Hannah Glasse, p. 368 (1753)

Rice Custard

1–2 pints boiled rice (depending on how custardy you wish)

4 cups cream

1 blade mace or ¼ teaspoon

2–4 tablespoons sugar (to taste)

1–2 tablespoons rose water

1. In a heavy saucepan, boil your cream with the mace gently.
2. In a bowl, beat the boiled rice, then add it to the cream, stirring constantly.
3. When well mixed and hot enough, take it off the heat, and add the sugar and rose water.
4. Let mixture cool, then plate, and serve.

Rice Pudding

Take a quarter of a pound of rice, put it into a saucepan, with a quart of new milk, a stick of cinnamon, and stir it often to prevent it sticking to the saucepan. When it is boiled thick, put it into a pan, stir in a quarter of a pound of fresh butter, and sugar it to the palate. Grate in half a nutmeg, add three or four spoonsful of rose water, and stir all well together. When cold, beat up eight eggs with half the whites, and then beat it all well together. Pour it into a buttered dish, and bake it.

—*The London Art of Cookery and Domestic Housekeepers' Complete Assistant*, John Farley, pp. 187-188 Puddings (1811)

Rice Pudding

5 tablespoons butter
2½ cups hot cooked rice
1 cup brown sugar
4 egg yolks, well beaten
2 egg whites, well beaten
2 cups milk
½ teaspoon nutmeg, grated
½ teaspoon cinnamon
¼ cup rose water

1. Stir the butter into the hot rice, and allow the mixture to cool to room temperature. Add the brown sugar.
2. In a separate bowl, beat together the eggs, milk, nutmeg, cinnamon, and rose water until well blended. Combine this mixture with the rice mixture.
3. Pour into a buttered 2½-quart baking dish. Bake in a 325°F oven for 1¼ hours or until done.

To Make a Very Good Cream

When you churn butter, take out half a pint of cream just as it begins to turn to butter, (that is, when it is a little frothy) then boil a quart of good thick and new cream, season it with sugar and a little rose-water, when it is quite cold, mingle it very well with that you take out of the churn, and so dish it.

—*The Accomplisht Cook, or,*
The Whole Art and Mystery of Cookery,
Fitted for All Degrees and Qualities,
Robert May, p. 283 (1685)

Rose Cream

3½ cups water
½ cup rose water
½ cup dry powdered milk
½ cup sugar
5 tablespoons + 1 teaspoon cornstarch
red food dye (optional)

1. Whisk the water, rose water, powdered milk, sugar, and cornstarch together in a saucepan until smooth.
2. Place over medium heat, stirring constantly with a wooden spoon. Cook until it begins to boil.
3. Cook at a gentle boil for 2 minutes.
4. Remove from heat immediately, stirring a few times to help it cool. (Optional—stir in one tiny drop of red dye to color cream.)
5. Pour into 8 small glasses or a mold.
6. Refrigerate until set, at least 2 hours.

Snow and Cream

Make a rich boiled custard and put it in the bottom of your china or glass dish, then take the whites of eight eggs beat with rose water and a spoonful of treble refined sugar, till it is a strong froth; put some milk and water into a broad stew pan, and when it boils take the froth off the eggs and lay it on the milk and water, and let it boil once up; take it off carefully, and lay it on your custard.

—*The Experienced English Housekeeper*,
Elizabeth Raffald, p. 254 (1784)

Snow and Cream

6 eggs, separated
1¼ cups milk
1¼ cups cream
2 tablespoons rose water
1½ tablespoons granulated sugar
6 egg whites

½ tablespoon rose water
2½ tablespoons confectioners' sugar
water and milk (combined—enough to cover
    1½-inch of the bottom of a frying pan)

To make the custard:
1. Whisk the egg yolks well. Then mix the yolks with milk, cream, and granulated sugar.
2. Gently and continuously stir this mixture over a very low heat in a heavy saucepan or in the top of a double boiler.
3. Add the rose water to taste. Once the mixture coats the back of a wooden spoon, remove from the heat immediately.
4. Pour the custard into a shallow serving dish or bowl, or fill glasses three-quarters full.
5. Cover with plastic wrap, and let cool.

To make the snow:
1. Whisk the egg whites very stiff, gradually adding the rose water and confectioners' sugar to make a meringue.
2. In a large, deep frying pan, combine milk and water until the liquid is 1½-inch deep. Bring to a simmer.
3. Add large spoonfuls (plum size) of the meringue to the milk-water.
4. Poach gently until firm underneath; then, using two spoons, carefully turn them over and lightly poach the other side.
5. Place snow mounds on the custard to serve.

An Almond Hedgehog
(see pg. 147)

Miscellaneous

This selection of interesting recipes doesn't quite fit into neat categories. Where else would you put marzipan hedgehogs with slivered almond spines (and currant eyes that look back at you), or a creamless custard called Buttered Oranges, or the eighteenth-century version of doughnut holes called German Puffs?

To Make a Hedgehog

Blanch a pound of almonds, beat them in a mortar very fine, with a little rose-water; put them in a stew-pan, with half a pint of cream, the yolks of six eggs, and the whites of three; grate in a rind of a lemon, and as much sugar as will sweeten it to your taste; stir it over a slow fire till it is thick; put it in a dish, and make it in the form of a hedge-hog; slice some almonds longways, and stick it all over to look like bristles; put round it a pint of boiled custard.

—*The Compleat Housewife; or,*
Accomplished Gentlewoman's Companion,
Eliza Smith, p. 316 (1728)

An Almond Hedgehog

1–2 (7-ounce) tubes of almond paste (depending on how large you wish to make your hedgehog)

½–1 teaspoon rose water

8–10 ounces slivered almonds

2 large currants or 2 small raisins (for the eyes)

1. Remove three-quarters of the almond paste from the foil tube, and begin to soften and work it in your hands with a little rose water until it forms a ball.
2. Begin to form the body of the hedgehog on a plate or flat surface.
3. Take most of the remaining almond paste and form the head. (Leave enough to make the ears.) Then attach the head to the body by blending the almond paste using a knife or a small skewer.
4. Attach the ears in the same manner, blending them into the head.
5. Attach the currants for eyes, and with your knife, make a small slit for a mouth.
6. Beginning at the neck, attach the almond slivers as quills all the way down the body.
7. If you wish, you may make a custard or cream (made with the cream, egg yolks, and sugar) to place around the hedgehog.

Note: If you wish, you may make a custard or cream to place around the hedgehog using the custard receipts from A Fine Cream on p.125, Portugal Cream, p.129, or the cream from the Snow and Cream receipt, p. 143.

To Make a Begger's Pudding

Take some stale Bread; pour over it some hot Water, till it is well soaked; then press out the Water, and wash the Bread; add some powdered Ginger, Nutmeg grated, and a little Salt; some Rosewater or Sack, some Lisbon Sugar, and some Currants; mix these well together, and lay it in a Pan well buttered on the Sides; and when it is well flatted with a Spoon, lay some Pieces of Butter on the Top; bake it in a gentle Oven, and serve it hot. You may turn it out of the Pan when it is cold, and it will eat like a fine Cheesecake.

—*Lady's Companion*, p. 51 (1733)

Begger's Pudding

butter

stale bread

hot water

1 teaspoon ginger

1 teaspoon nutmeg

pinch salt

1 tablespoon rose water (or sack)

½–1 cup sugar (to taste)

½–1 cup currants

1. Generously butter the sides of a baking dish.
2. Place stale bread in the baking dish. Pour hot water over it until soaked.
3. Press the water out of the bread.
4. In a separate bowl, mix the ginger, nutmeg, salt, rose water (or sack), sugar, and currants together. Pour over the bread.
5. Flatten the bread with a spoon.
6. Lay some pieces of butter on top.
7. Bake at 300°F for about 20 minutes or until the bread begins to look baked.

To Make Black Caps

TAKE six large apples, and cut a slice off the blossom end, put them in a tin, and set them in a quick oven till they are brown, then wet them with rose water, and grate a little sugar over them, and set them in the oven again till they look bright, and very black, then take them out, and put them into a deep china dish or plate, and pour round them thick cream custard, or white wine and sugar.

—*The Experienced English Housekeeper*,
Elizabeth Raffald, p. 206 (1776)

Black Caps

6 large apples

¼–½ cup rose water

1–2 tablespoons sugar (to taste)

custard or a white wine and sugar sauce

1. Place the apples in a deep pan.
2. Put in a preheated 375°F oven until they begin to turn brown.
3. Remove the pan from the oven, and pour the rose water over the apples. Then sprinkle the sugar over them.
4. Return the pan to the oven, baking until the apples are dark and the skin begins to split.
5. Remove the apples from the oven, place in a deep dish, and pour the custard or white wine and sugar sauce all around before serving.

A White Wine Sauce

(for 4 apples)

2 cups Sugar

⅔–1 cup white wine

1. Place the sugar and the white wine in a saucepan
2. On medium heat, stir the sugar and wine together until the sugar is dissolved
3. Pour this sauce over the baked apples

Note: If you wish, you may make a custard or cream to pour around the Black Caps using the custard receipts from A Fine Cream on page 125, Portugal Cream, page 129, or the cream from the Snow and Cream receipt, page 143.

Bread and Butter Pudding

Take a penny French roll two day old, cut off all the crust, and cut the crumb into thin slices, spreading it as you cut it very thin with butter on each slice; then take a quarter of a pound of raisins stoned, half a pound of currants well washed and picked; then lay a layer of bread and butter, and upon that fruit in a pudding-dish, so cover the fruit with buttered bread, and when it is disposed of into your dish, beat up five eggs with a quart of new milk, sweeten it to your taste, and put to it a glass of rose-water, pour it into the dish upon the bread and fruit, and bake it an hour.

—*Every Woman Her Own Housekeeper*,
John Perkins, p. 288 (1796)

Bread and Butter Pudding

This is a half recipe for an 8- or 9-inch baking dish.

French bread (⅓–½ loaf), two days old
½ cup currants
½ cup raisins
2 medium eggs + 1 large egg
2 cups milk
⅓ cup sugar
2 tablespoons rose water

1. Cut the crust off the French bread. Slice it into thin slices, and butter each side.
2. Place a layer of the bread in the bottom of your pudding bowl, and sprinkle some of the currants and raisins on the bread.
3. Continue to alternate a layer of bread and then some fruit until the dish is full.
4. In a bowl, beat the eggs with the milk.
5. Add sugar and rose water to the milk and egg mixture.
6. Pour the milk and egg mixture gently over the bread and fruit.
7. Bake at 350°F for 50 minutes. Then, keeping the door shut, turn the oven off and leave the pudding in for another 5 minutes.

Buttered Oranges

Take eight Eggs, and the Whites of four; beat them well together, then squeeze into them the Juice of seven good Oranges, and three or four Spoonfuls of Rose-water, and let them run through a Hair-Sieve into a Silver Bason; then put to it half a Pound of Sugar beaten, set it over a gentle Fire, and when it begins to thicken, put in a Bit of Butter, about the Bigness of a large Nutmeg, and when it is somewhat thicker pour it into a broad flat China Dish, and eat it cold. It will not keep very well above two Days, but is very wholesome and pleasant to the taste.

—*The Housekeeper's Pocket Book*,
Sarah Harrison, p. 159 (1760)

Buttered Oranges

This is a half recipe.

4 medium egg yolks + 2 whites
½ cup sugar
1½ cups orange juice
2½ teaspoons rose water
2 tablespoons butter

1. Beat the egg yolks, egg whites, and sugar together. Beat in the orange juice and rose water.
2. In the top of a double boiler, cook the mixture until it starts to thicken.
3. Cut the butter into small pieces, and add it to the mixture.
4. Cook it gently until the mixture is thick enough to coat a metal spoon.
5. Pour the custard into a bowl, and refrigerate.

German Puffs

Put half a pint of good milk into a tossing pan, and dredge in flour till it is thick as hasty pudding, keep stirring it over a slow fire till it is all of a lump, then put it in a marble mortar, when it is cold put to it the yolks of eight eggs, four ounces of sugar, a spoonful of rose-water, grate a little nutmeg, and the rind of half a lemon, beat them together an hour or more, when it looks light and bright, drop them into a pan of boiling lard with a tea spoon, the size of a large nutmeg, they will rise and look like a large yellow plum if they are well beat: as you fry them, lay them on a sieve to drain, grate sugar round your dish, and serve them up with sack for sauce.

—*The Experienced Housekeeper*,
Elizabeth Raffald, p. 164 (1776)

German Puffs

This is a half recipe.

½ cup milk

¼ cup flour

4 egg yolks

4 tablespoons (2 ounces) sugar

¼ teaspoon rose water

a few sprinkles nutmeg

half a rind of a lemon

shortening or lard for boiling

sugar to dust

1. Place milk into a heavy saucepan, and dredge the flour into it until it is as thick as hasty pudding, like a light doughnut or fritter batter.
2. Put the heavy saucepan over a low flame on your stove. Continue stirring it until it forms a ball.
3. Let the flour and milk ball cool. Once it is cold, add the egg yolks, sugar, rose water, a little grated nutmeg, and the rind of half a lemon. Beat this mixture until it is light.
4. Bring your lard or shortening to a boil.
5. With a teaspoon, drop large walnut-sized pieces of batter into the oil.
6. The batter will rise and become yellow in color; at this point, they are done. Remove them from the oil, and lay them on paper to drain. Sprinkle some sugar over them, and serve.

You can make a dipping sauce with sack (sherry) if you like.

March-Pane

TAKE a pound of Jordan almonds, blanch and beat them in a marble mortar very fine; then put to them three quarters of a pound of double-refin'd sugar, and beat them with a few drops of orange-flower-water; beat all together till 'tis a very good Paste, then roll it into what shape you please; dust a little fine sugar under it as you roll it, to keep it from sticking. To ice it, search double-refined sugar as fine as flour, wet it with rose-water, and mix it well together, and with a brush or a bunch of feathers spread it over you March-pane: Bake them in an oven that is not too hot; put wafer-paper at the bottom, and white paper under that, so keep them for use.

—*The Compleat Housewife; or,*
Accomplished Gentlewoman's
Companion, Eliza Smith, p. 148 (1739)

March-Pane (Marzipan)

1¼ cups ground blanched almonds (approx. 1½ cups whole blanched almonds)
1½ cups sugar
3½ teaspoons orange-flower water

Icing
¼ cup confectioners' sugar
4 teaspoons rose water

1. Preheat oven to 225°F. Line a baking sheet with parchment paper.
2. Mix almonds and sugar in a food processor on low speed. Gradually add the orange-flower water, and beat until this mixture forms a crumbly paste.
3. Knead the paste with your hands until the ingredients are evenly incorporated.
4. Shape by hand, or press this mixture into candy molds, and turn onto your baking sheet.
5. To make the icing, dissolve the confectioners' sugar in the rose water.
6. With a pastry brush, brush the icing mixture onto the tops of the marzipan, wait a few minutes, and repeat until you have applied four layers.
7. Bake for 55 minutes. Cool on a wire rack.

Plain Ice Cream

Put one pint of cream into a freezing pot in a little ice, whisk it about till it hangs about the whisk; then take the whisk out and put as much powdered sugar as will lay on half a crown; stir it and scrape it about with your ice scraper till you find it all frozen; put it into your moulds and put them into your ice to take the shape.

—*The Complete Confectioner; or The Whole Art of Confectionary*, by a person, late an apprentice to the well-known Mssrs. Negri and Witten, (London, 1760)

Rose Petal Ice Cream

4 heaping tablespoons dark red rose petals

1½ tablespoons caster sugar

4 fluid ounces red dessert wine

4 fluid ounces double or heavy cream

3 tablespoons confectioners' sugar

2 egg whites

1. Place the petals, caster sugar, and wine in a food processor, and combine until liquid.
2. In a separate bowl, beat the cream with the confectioner's sugar until it is thick.
3. Stir the rose mixture into the cream mixture.
4. In a separate bowl, beat the egg whites until stiff, then fold into the cream. Put this combined mixture into an ice cream maker, turn on per maker's instructions. Once frozen, store in freezer, or serve immediately.

Glace de Roses

Pound a handful of roses, and pour a pint of hot Water upon them, let them infuse about an hour, adding about half a pound of sugar-, when it is properly dissolved, sift through a Napkin. . . . different infusions are also mixed with Cream instead of Water.

—The Professed Cook,
B. Claremont, pp. 596-597 (1776)

Rose Water Ices

2 cups fragrant rose petals
1 cup + 2 tablespoons superfine sugar
3 cups cold water
3 tablespoons fresh lemon juice
1 cup sparkling wine

1. Cut the triangular colored base from each rose petal.
2. Place the rose petals and sugar in a food processor; mix until smooth. Occasionally scrape down sides.
3. Add ½ cup of water. Blend for a few seconds.
4. Add the remaining water, lemon juice, and sparkling wine. Blend.
5. Filter mixture through a sieve.
6. Place mixture in an ice cream maker, and follow the maker's instructions.
7. Store in freezer to harden.

Westminster Fool

Take a Penny Loaf, cut it into thin Slices, wet them with Sack, lay them in the Bottom of a Dish: Take a Quart of Cream, beat up six Eggs, two Spoonfuls of Rose Water, a Blade of Mace, and some Grated Nutmeg. Sweeten to your Taste. Put this all into a Sauce-pan, and keep stirring all the Time over a slow Fire for fear of curdling. When it begins to be thick, pour it into the Dish over the Bread; let it stand till it is cold, and serve it up.

—The Art of Cookery Plain and Easy,
Hannah Glasse, p. 153 (1747)

Westminster Fool

This is a half recipe.

bread (Italian or French bread, as much as fits in the bottom of your baking dish)
⅓ cup (or to taste) sack
2 cups cream
3 large eggs, beaten
1½ teaspoons rose water
generous pinch mace
½ teaspoon ground nutmeg
¼ cup sugar

1. Cut the bread into thin slices. Layer the bread in a dish, and pour some sack over it until the bread is fully saturated, but not so soggy it falls apart.
2. In a saucepan, combine the cream, eggs, rose water, mace, nutmeg, and sugar. Stir constantly over a low flame. Do not allow the mixture to curdle.
3. When the mixture thickens, take it off the flame, and pour it over the bread in the dish.
4. Let it stand until it is cold; then serve.

A Whitpot

Cut half a loaf of bread in slices, pour thereon 2 quarts
milk, 6 eggs, rose-water, nutmeg, and half pound of sugar;
put into dish and cover with paste. No. 1*. Bake slow
1 hour.

*Paste No. 1

Rub one pound of butter into one pound of flour, whip
2 whites and add with cold water and one yolk; make
into paste, roll in six or seven times one pound of butter,
flowering it each roll. This is good for any small thing.

—*American Cookery*,
Amelia Simmons, p. 26 (1796)

Whitpot

This is a half recipe.

¼ loaf bread (French or Italian, sliced)

2 pints milk

3 eggs

2½ tablespoons rose water

1 teaspoon nutmeg

1 cup sugar

1. Cut the loaf of bread into thin slices, and place in a baking dish.
2. In a bowl, combine the milk, eggs, rose water, nutmeg, and sugar. Whisk until blended.
3. Pour the egg mixture over the bread.
4. Make a pie crust (see Paste No. 1 on previous page), and place it over the top of the mixture.
5. Bake at 350°F for 1 hour.

Black Caps (see pg. 151)

Glossary of Common Eighteenth-century Terms

coddle	To poach or steam in a covered pan
do.	Abbreviation for *ditto*
fair (of water)	Clean; pure
jack	Half the size of a gill
gill or jill	Exclusively a liquid measure (in the United States = ½ cup or 4 fluid ounces) In Great Britain = 5 fluid ounces or ¼ pint
hoop	Open-ended pan for baking. Parchment needs to be tied around one end.
manchet	Finest wheaten bread
papers	Parchment
penny loaf	Small bread bun which costs a penny. The size of the loaf could vary depending on the prevailing cost of the flour used in baking.
pippin	A variety of apple
q.s.	(quantum suffict) as much as suffices
routs	Great assemblies or parties
sack	White fortified wine imported from Spain or the Canary Islands = *sherry*
searce	To sieve
strains	The white threads on egg yolks
tins	Baking sheets

March-Pane (Marzipan)
(see pg. 159)

Eighteenth-century Oven Temperature Conversions

	Temps °F	Temps °C
Cool oven	200–275°F	(90°C)
Slow oven	300–325°F	(150–160°C)
Moderate oven	350–375°F	(180–190°C)
Hot oven	400–450°F	(200–230°C)
Quick oven	375–400°F	(190–200°C)
Very slow oven	below 300°F	(below 140 °C)

Bibliography

A Person, *The Whole Art of Confectionary* (London)

Anonymous, *Lady's Companion* (1733)

Acworth, Margaretta, *Georgian Cookery Book,* reprinted by Pavilion Books Limited (Great Britain, 1987)

Barry, Michael, *Recipes from the Great Houses,* (Past Times, Oxford, England, 1996)

Beebe, Ruth Anne, *Sallets, Humbles & Shrewsbery Cakes* (David R. Godine Publisher, New Hampshire, 1976)

Black, Maggie, *Georgian Meals & Menus,* (Kingsmead Press, Bath, England, 1977)

Bradley, Martha, *The British Housewife; or, the Cook, Housekeeper's, and Gardiner's Companion* (London, 1756), facsimile reprint (Prospect Books, London, 1996)

By a Person, Late an Apprentice to the well-known Mssrs. Negri and Witten, *The Complete Confectioner; or the Whole Art of Confectionary* (London, 1760)

Carter, Charles, *The Compleat Practical Cook* (London, 1730)

Carter Crump, Nancy, *Hearthside Cooking*, (EPM Publications, Virginia, 1986)

Claremont, B., *The Professed Cook* (1776)

Crane, Fanny Pierson, *Her Receipts 1796, Confections, Savouries and Drams* (1796)

Day, Ivan, *Daily Life through History, Cooking in Europe 1650-1850* (Greenwood Press, 2009)

De la Falaise, Maxime, *Seven Centuries of English Cooking* (Barnes & Noble, New York, 1973)

DiMarco, Vincent, *Egg Pies, Moss Cakes, and Pigeons Like Puffins, Eighteenth-Century British Cookery from Manuscript Sources* (iUniverse, Inc., 2007)

Dubourcq, Hilaire, *Benjamin Franklin Book of Recipes*, (London, 2004)

Farley, John, *The London Art of Cookery and Domestic Housekeeper's Complete Assistant* (12th Edition, London, 1811, reprinted by Applewood Books, Bedford, Massachusetts)

Glasse, Hannah, *The Art of Cookery Made Plain and Easy* (Dublin 1758) (London 1747, 1753, 1762, 1768, 1778, 1796)

Glasse, Hannah, *The Complete Confectioner: or, the Whole Art of Confectionary Made Plain and Easy* (London, 1742, 1760)

Harkness, J. L., *The World's Favorite Roses and How to Grow Them*, (McGraw-Hill Book Company, New York, 1979)

Harrison, Sarah, *The Housekeeper's Pocket Book* (1738, 1760)

Henderson, W. A., *The Housekeeper's Instructor or, Universal Family Cook* (14th edition, 1807)

Hess, Karen, *Martha Washington's Booke of Cookery*, reprinted by Columbia University Press (New York, 1995)

Ignotus, *Culina Famulatrix Medicinae: or Receipts in Modern Cookery; with a Medical Commentary* (York, England, 1806)

Kidder, Edward. E. Kidder's *Receipts of Pastry and Cookery for the Use of His Scholars* (London, 1720)

Kikball, Marie, *The Martha Washington Cook Book* (Tresco Publishers, Canton, Ohio, 1940)

Martin, Clair G., *100 Old Roses for the American Garden*, (Workman Publishing, 1999)

May, Robert, *The Accomplisht Cook, or, the Whole Art and Mystery of Cookery, Fitted for All Degrees and Qualities.* (1685)

McWilliams, James E., *A Revolution in Eating, How the Quest for Food Shaped America* (Columbia University Press, New York, 2005)

Moxon, Elizabeth, *English Housewifery* (London, 1775), (Edinburgh, 1790)

Norwak, Mary, *East Anglian Recipes: 300 Years of Housewife's Choice,* (Larks Press, Norfolk, England, 1996)

Paston-Williams, Sara, *The Art of Dining* (the National Trust, London, 1993)

Pelton, Robert W., *Baking Receipts from the Wives & Mothers of Our Founding Fathers* (Infinity Publishing, Pennsylvania, 2004)

Perkins, John, *Every Woman Her Own Housekeeper* (1796)

Raffald, Elizabeth, *The Experienced English Housekeeper, for the Use and Ease of Ladies, Housekeepers, Cooks, &c.* (London, 1776, 1782)

Richardson, Rosamond, *Roses - A Celebration*, (Piatkus Publishers, London, 1984)

Rundell, Maria, *Domestic Cookery for Private Families* (1806)

Sambrook, Pamela A. and Brears, Peter, *The Country House Kitchen 1650-1900* (The History Press, Gloucestershire, England, 2010)

Sherman, Sandra, *Fresh from the Past* (Taylor Trade Publishing, Lanham, Maryland, 2004)

Simmons, Amelia, *American Cookery: or, the Art of Dressing Viands, Fish, Poultry and Vegetables and the Best Mode of Making Puff-Pastes, Pies, Tarts, Puddings, Custards and Preserves, and All Kinds of Cakes*, facsimile of the second edition (Albany, New York, 1796)

Smith, Eliza, *The Compleat Housewife; or, Accomplished Gentlewoman's Companion* (London, 1728, 1739)

Stead, Jennifer. *Food and Cooking in 18th Century Britain* (English Heritage, 1985)

Verrall, William, *William Verrall's Cookery Book 1759*, Introduction by Colin Brent, (Southover Press, East Sussex, England, 1988)

Acknowledgments

This book came about due to the enthusiasm and encouragement of a number of individuals.

To my best friend, Honey Berman, you literally pushed, prodded, and got me to finish this book. You always believed in me. Thank you for your support but most of all for your loving friendship.

To my right hand and assistant through all this, Stephanie Deal Nacionales, you are terrific! When I began to go "mad scientist," Steph was right behind me saying, "Did you just put another ¼ teaspoon in without recording it?" Lo and behold, she had already put it into my recipe notes. Steph had my back for most of this book. Once again, I am grateful for her friendship and interest in my experimental eighteenth-century baking.

To Myriam Hu, you were there at the beginning of my rose-water experiments. Your knowledge of roses was invaluable. You made the early experiments such fun! It was you who got me through making 1,800 rose cookies for the Great Rosarians, laughing all the way as you rolled cookie dough with chopsticks faster than I could with a tablespoon. You have been a dear friend and my "big sister" for a number of years. I treasure your friendship.

Grateful thanks go to my sister-in-law Julia, who taught me how to make the most wonderful pie crust!

To all my taste testers; Jonathan, Honey, Ted, Bob, Valencia, Linda, Lynda, Melanie, Meagan, Katelyn, Maurissa, Elizabeth, Marc, DJ, Andrea, Mel, and the entire crew at my Chase Bank, as well as from the Huntington Library; Clair, Melanie, Danni, and Cynthia. Your comments and support have been invaluable. Thank you.

To Victoria Zackheim, who graciously introduced an untested author to her literary agent, I thank you for your kindness and generosity of spirit.

To my agent, Jill Marsal, thank you for taking a chance on me. I appreciate all your efforts for a first-time author. It is a pleasure working with you.

To Bonnie Matthews, whose keen eye and good spirit made the final photo session such fun!

Many thanks to Clair Martin for allowing and encouraging me to experiment while he was curator at The Huntington Library and Gardens. Clair was also one of my finest taste testers. His kindness, rose expertise, and fine palate were an immense help in refining these rose receipts.

I'd also like to thank Jim Folsom, Director of the Botanical Gardens at the Huntington Library and Gardens for encouraging me to use the botanical research library.

Thank you to my sister Phyllis and my nephew Jeremy for their love and support.

Finally, I want to thank my wonderful husband, Radford. Your love, patience, and sense of humor have sustained me for almost forty years. You are my partner, my love, and my hero. Who else would have tasted dozens of rose desserts, photographed these desserts, and showed infinite patience at my computer skills? You have always been there for me, and I love you with all my heart.

To learn more about Judy and her work, please visit https://ensign33.wordpress.com.

Index